A CHANCE TO FIND THE SUNSHINE

That's all those young people needed. A chance to live! A chance to love! And someone to listen!

Ron Keller is one who has heard the cry of today's lonely generation, and has decided to give them the chance they need.

HOLD ON TILL MORNING

by RON KELLER

Whitaker House
504 LAUREL DRIVE, MONROEVILLE, PA 15146

Cover illustration by Rudy Falsetti

ISBN: 0-88368-051-3

WHITAKER HOUSE
504 Laurel Drive
Monroeville, Pennsylvania 15146

Some of the names in this book have been changed to protect the individuals involved. The events are absolutely as described.

Unless otherwise indicated, all Scripture quotations are from The Jerusalem Bible, © 1966 by Darton, Longman & Tod, Ltd. and Doubleday & Company, Inc. Used by permission of the publisher.

To my wife,
my family,
Young Life,
and others involved
in my spiritual journey.

TABLE OF CONTENTS

Foreword

What you're about to read is an intensely human story. God's grace is the only explanation for how it happened.

Why it happened is another story.

The "why" is probably best explained by the book you now hold in your hand. It is God's medium for relaying a message meant especially for *you*.

The author shares how he searched, suffered and finally succeeded in a quest for that which we all desire. He's put it in print that we too might make the discovery.

The book is short. It's stirring. It's well worth the investment of your time. I believe this is especially true if you're a parent or involved in youth work of any kind.

So sit back and relax. Let the Spirit speak to your heart.

Larry Tomczak
Author of *Clap Your Hands!*

PREFACE

Michel Montaigne, born in 1533, was a man of insatiable intellectual curiosity. In 1580 he published the first book of essays ever written—and it is still being reprinted. Montaigne quoted copiously. He wrote:

"Anyone who would like to know the sources of the verses and examples I have piled up here would put me to great trouble to tell him.... I gather the flowers by the wayside, by the brooks and in the meadows, and only the string with which I bind them together is my own."

These are my sentiments about the borrowed ideas that are contained in this book. Only the "string" of my own experiences ties them together in an arrangement that I hope will be fresh.

I do not claim for this book any deep scholarly qualities. This is not a book on doctrines, dogma, creeds or "churchianity." Many such books are available, and some of them are excellent. I have read few books, however, that deal with the experiences of practical men—men who seek to know and experience more of a God Who transcends all theological speculation.

In recent times, there has been increasing conflict between those Christians who are experientially-oriented and those who are intellectually-oriented. It is a conflict that may never be resolved. In the final analysis, however, the one who speaks with the most authority is the one who has "been there."

In some ways, Christianity can be compared with marriage. It is one thing to intellectualize about marriage but quite another thing to experience it. Like marriage, the Christian Faith is essentially an experience—a relationship with a person—not a concept, idea, creed, formula, philosophy or theology.

Others can talk and write about that relationship much more fluently than I. What really counts, however, is that God and what He has done be presented very clearly. In this book I have simply told about one man's encounter with God and my interpretation of that encounter. For the reader who has also encountered God, or who is seeking Him, the inadequacies of my words and style of writing will be of little importance.

Chapter 1

Fear not that thy
life shall come to
an end,
but
rather, fear that
it shall never
have a
beginning.
     Cardinal Newman

"The Young Punk"

The first fifteen years of my life were frittered away in Strasburg, North Dakota, a small, predominantly German-Catholic community. We had the usual Podunk-town facilities: the local creamery, the one-man post office, the big Catholic church (and a couple of smaller, Protestant ones), the barber shop, the police station, the grocery store, a few restaurants, and far too many taverns.

Strasburg's only claim to distinction is that it is Lawrence Welk's home town. When I lived there, the town was made up largely of middle-middle and lower-middle class families. The older residents could vaguely recollect their pilgrimage to America from their European "homeland." The older, German families lived in one area of town, the newer arrivals in another.

Strasburg's social life was sluggish. The older people for the most part were content with gossiping and playing cards. The "younger generation" craved more excitement, and many of us began smoking and drinking in our very early years. I was only seven or eight years old when I smoked my first cigarette, but I didn't gain the distinction of getting "plastered" until I was ten. Before that time, however, I had had my share of nips and samples.

When we became bored with smoking "snitched" cigarettes and drinking stolen, homemade wines, we usually checked out girls. Since the boys I hung around with were older than I, I found myself in the company of older girls. This seemed to me an enviable position, until I happened to hear two of my "girlfriends" whispering about the young punk that they always had to hang around with. I was crushed—and for awhile after that, avoided girls.

Our town had the usual pizza joints and other hangouts for teenagers. When I was in the seventh grade, a friend and I discovered how to rig the toughest pinball machine in the most popular hangout. By drilling a hole in the side and inserting a clothes hanger, we managed to make the machine rack up five, ten, and fifteen extra games. Then one day the tough manager caught us. That ended my "career" in outsmarting the pinballs. I ended up sitting outside the cafe (even in winter) while my friends enjoyed the profits from my "rigging" technique inside.

In my crowd, pulling off pranks was the "in" thing to do. Whoever could think up the meanest and dirtiest trick and carry it out without getting caught was the lion of the group. I was one of the ringleaders.

It was my desire for recognition that led me to do all those bad things. I was seldom very good at doing anything constructive. Every time I went out for basketball or other sports, I would either get caught smoking or would just give up because my friends told me that basketball was for sissies. My father felt the same way, so I didn't get much encouragement to be an athlete from him or anyone else.

Our family lived across the street from the Catholic grade school I attended. On our side of the block was the house where the Sisters of Notre Dame lived; on the other side was our garage and an open lot out behind it that we used for playing football and for riding go-carts, bikes, and motor scooters. That lot was a frequent meeting place for the in crowd of outcasts: those who didn't make good grades or athletic teams. Hidden from our parents behind the garage, we would smoke cigarettes, speculate about sex, and discuss our predicaments.

My parents never liked my friends. They always thought—with good reason—that I was being led into things that would get me into trouble. How they ever learned about our activities, I'll never know. My father, especially, was very suspicious. A short, bespectacled man with bushy hair and an ever-present cigarette hanging out of his mouth, he rarely smiled at anyone. Maybe he thought smiles and authority didn't mix. After all, he *was* part-time deputy (as well as part-time printer), and he played that role with an intensity, even in our home.

Because of my father's drinking problem, Mom had to take on odd jobs to support the family. Young and good looking, tall and talkative, she seemed the very opposite of my father. Often both of them were away from home until late at night. I remember sobbing myself to sleep many nights when my father was out patrolling the town and my mother was at work. I hated the feeling of being responsible for the younger children—Don, Kathy and Dick. From the moment my parents left until late in the evening, we scrapped about all kinds of things. After we finally stopped fighting and went to bed, we were often awakened later by the noise of another fight—this time between our parents. We kids were terrified for mother when this happened, and Don and I would rush out to the kitchen to try to protect her from our father's drunken rage.

Our family had one thing going for us—our relatives. Although they lived in other parts of the country (New York, Minneapolis, and Seattle), they were always standing by to help us out in times of need. And we had plenty of those times. When my grandparents came to visit, they were usually loaded down with clothes and other gifts. My godmother and aunts frequently mailed or brought presents to us children. My uncles usually gave us things that they knew we'd never get otherwise: games, toys, and musical instruments.

I was thankful for these big-hearted relatives, and was encouraged by their kindness and their obvious sympathy for Mom and us kids.

Almost everyone who visited Strasburg noticed the church bells. They rang at least three or four times a day (more often when there were funerals or weddings), and could be heard for miles around. To the older folks, the sound of the bells was comforting and reassuring. They seemed to say, "All is well; what you people are doing is pleasing to God and your fellow man."

To me, the church bells were a pain in the neck. They usually meant, "It's time to go home," or "It's time to go to church."

As long as I was in grade school, I was compelled to go to church. Almost all the other Catholic families I knew were the same. My father laid down the law about us going to church, but it was Mom who got up and took us. We went to church every Sunday and every holy day. We participated in communion, confession, confirmation and all the other religious exercises, hoping that these things would earn us life after death.

Our church was one of the old-time Catholic churches, colorfully painted and elaborately decorated with gold trim. It had a hundred-foot steeple, a colossal choir loft, a golden-throated pipe organ, and an elaborate altar. Statues of saints were everywhere. I remember asking, one day in church, "Mom, what are all these statues for?"

"To help you pray," she replied.

"But how do they help you pray?"

"They help you concentrate on God," was her impatient answer.

I think I responded by telling her that they didn't have that effect on me.

When I was attending confirmation class at the age of twelve, the Sister who was instructing us told each of us to choose some saint whom we thought could be our hero in life. I remember struggling for a name. We were supposed to know a lot about the saints of the Church, but I was unable to come up with a name. So the Sister assigned me one: Saint Benedict. I hated to tell her that I already had a saint. Elvis Presley was making it big in those days, and Saint Benedict couldn't hold a candle to him.

Being a "good Catholic," however, I accepted the venerable name, learned about Saint Benedict, and assured Sister Thomas of my intention to be just like him, beard and all.

I'll never know why Sister Thomas and Sister Isabel proposed me as a mass-server. It was a great honor to be chosen for this office, since servers were somewhat more holy than other boys.

By the time winter came, however, I wasn't sure that all this holiness was worth the effort. When the temperatures were thirty below zero and the wind was howling at thirty to forty miles per hour, getting up at 6:00 A.M. to serve Mass quickly lost its attraction. I began to question whether religion had any value at all, and I found myself wishing, even while I was serving mass that I'd soon be old enough (like Dad) to junk this religious crap. I hated the processions, the candles, the smell of incense, the wax on my cassock, and the meetings in the church basement. I was enough of a hypocrite to conceal my thoughts from the priest, however, and they never found out about the frequent arguments I had with my mother before I went to serve.

I didn't understand much of what took place in church, and out of boredom, I spent most of my time thinking up tricks to play on fellow servers. Several times Father Michael or Father Stephen caught me doing something outrageous and gave me a spanking that I didn't soon forget. Both of them had strong right hands that had cast many a fishing line.

But whenever I got into grave trouble, as I did rather frequently for a grade-school boy, I would sneak into the church to visit God. I was afraid to be alone in the dark, and I never did stay long when I went in. But I always felt better after I left.

Like most Catholic boys, I was often urged by my grandmother to give the priesthood some consideration. Occasionally I had fantasies about living an easy life in a rectory, saying Mass, and hearing confessions.

Once in awhile, the kids in our neighborhood would "play Mass." The part I liked best was "playing confession," especially when it was my turn to be the priest. It was fun hearing the kids confess their sins, and it was also comforting when some other boy had a list of wicked deeds similar to my own.

Chapter 2

> *Nothing, I repeat, nothing*
> *about me is right;*
> *my general appearance, my character,*
> *my manners are discussed from A to Z.*
> *I'm expected (by order) to*
> *simply swallow all the harsh words and shouts*
> *in silence and I am not*
> *used to this. In fact, I can't. I'm not*
> *going to take all these insults*
> *lying down; I'll show them that Anne*
> *Frank wasn't born yesterday.*

> —*Anne Frank: The Diary of a*
> *Young Girl*, Otto H. Frank.
> Doubleday and Company,
> Garden City, N.Y. 1952, P.
> 43, by permission.

"Your Father is Sick."

All through grade school, I was greatly influenced by my family, my relatives, friends, school, and church. In my teen years, only a few relatives, a handful of friends, and my employers carried any weight with me. The church, the school, and my home had been written off as representing something I didn't need. In the crowd I ran with, rebelling against authority—especially parental authority—was the in thing to do.

Wanting to assert my independence, I sought ways to demonstrate that I could make it on my own. My parents were one step ahead of me. Instead of disagreeing with me, they advised me to go ahead in that kind of thinking—all the way. That meant I had to find a job, pay "rent" to help with family expenses, buy my own clothes, and raise my own spending money.

This was a pretty tough assignment for a

sophomore in high school, but I accepted the challenge. At fifteen, I began working in a small cream store. I got many a king-sized backache; unloading the hundred-pound cans of cream that the farmers brought in on truck wasn't exactly my idea of a white collar job. Later, I got a job as a trucker's helper on a milk pick-up route. That wasn't any better.

My teen years were years of fidgeting, searching, hurting, rejection, fear, and loneliness. The problems I had to face and the decisions I had to make were too numerous and too ovewhelming for a teen-ager.

The teen years are seldom easy, but my adolescence was complicated by my father's continued drinking, the discord between my parents, and our economic problems. I badly needed someone to talk to. I felt like I was headed for trouble, and I wanted to get straightened out before it was too late. I needed what every teen-ager needs: *a friend*. Not a counselor, teacher, administrator, parent, or pastor—but a real, listening friend. Someone a little older than I. Someone not too far removed from my experiences.

From time to time, my Uncle Joe came from Minneapolis and tried to fill the bill as best he could. I'll always love him for the interest he showed in me and the encouragement he gave me. He realized that there is a point in a kid's life where someone from outside the home must help. Whenever he could, he spent time with me in my early high school years.

When I was a junior in high school, I arrived home from school one day to find my mother in a state of melancholy. Usually she managed to conceal the anxiety and grief that my father's drinking caused her. Occasionally, though, her sorrow was so overwhelming that we could read it on her face. This was one of those rare times.

Poor Mom! She worked so hard—all the time. Besides raising four kids and holding a full-time job, she took on extra work like teaching piano lessons and proofreading manuscripts. We kids helped some—but we didn't really understand what a heavy burden Mom had to carry.

Only occasionally did we talk about Dad at home. When he was gone, we simply put him out of our minds and enjoyed the peace. But this day Mom felt the need to talk.

"Ron," she said as I walked into the kitchen, "I think we're going to have to do something about your father. He is really sick and needs special care—care that we can't give him. Can you understand that?" She looked at me anxiously and I nodded my head, not knowing what to expect next.

"We've tried everything—everything possible—but he won't quit drinking. Do you know what I mean?" Again I nodded, munching on a homemade chocolate chip cookie in an effort to appear casual.

Apologetically she continued, "I didn't want to do it, but I felt something had to be done. Things can't go on this way anymore." I saw tears beginning to form in the corners of her eyes. She usually ran to the bedroom when she cried, but this time she stayed right there with me.

"Today—" she went on, "today, your uncle and I signed some papers—papers to have your father committed to the state hospital and taken in for treatment. They came to get him a little while ago. Do you understand what I'm saying to you?"

Once more I nodded. "How long will he be there?" I asked, struggling to keep my voice steady.

"He needs a lot of help. Maybe a month, six months—maybe even longer." There was a pause before she could continue.

"He's been at this place before, Ron, and the treatment program has never worked. But this time—this time, I have more hopes because he can't leave until they let him go."

I recalled the high hopes we'd had for him when he came home after previous treatments—hopes that were dashed within a few hours. Almost before we had welcomed him home, he had left the house and returned to his favorite bar. Then, as if treatment had never happened, he was back on the bottle.

Understanding of my mother's tremendous emotional burden was slowly beginning to dawn on me. The solitary nights spent waiting for Dad to stagger home, her concern for us kids, feeding us, clothing us, and paying the rent; her worries about the family's future, my father's health, our family image. Suddenly I began to see the situation through her eyes—and I realized for the first time that her problems might be greater than mine.

Because I didn't want Mom to see me cry, I walked away, into the living room. As the tears that began deep inside started to surface, I ran upstairs to the room I shared with my brother. I missed my dad. I wanted him to be home. Even though he hadn't done much for or with me (and I hated him for that), I still missed him. I wanted our family to be happy, and I felt like running away because it wasn't. I knew my mother needed me. I wanted to prove I loved her. So I stayed.

After I had wept until no more tears would come, I went to the church. Alone in the cold and the dark, I sat surrounded by the beautiful decor, the statues, and the smell of incense. I didn't speak out loud, but in my mind I kept repeating the questions: "God, why do You make my dad drink? Why is he an alcoholic? God, why does my mother have to suffer so much?" I finally got up the courage to say what I really felt: "God, I don't like You."

I left the church feeling a little better. Finding my brothers and my sister at home, I took upon myself the responsibility of explaining the situation to them. They seemed to understand, and I felt better after telling them. I believe I grew up more in those few hours of sharing with my mother, sister and brothers than I had in the first fifteen years of my life. In a way, it made me feel good that Mom had taken me into her confidence. I began to feel a sense of responsibility for the family. It was at this point in my life that I made a simple choice to accept myself and our predicament, as bad as it was.

It seemed like a thousand years before we finally got any word about my father's condition. As Mother had expected, the doctors told us he would need long-range help. How long, no one knew.

Soon after my father's commitment to the hospital, Mom and Uncle Joe decided that our family might be better off in a larger town, where my father's condition wasn't known. During the summer, she found a job in Bismarck, and we moved into a small, overcrowded apartment in an unfamiliar city.

I wondered why Mom didn't let Dad know about our move, but Mom kept saying that if he loved us, he'd find us—if he ever got out of the hospital. I think I understood the anguish of heart that made her say that.

When fall came, I was enrolled in the local Catholic high school. The first few days in the hallways, I was scared. I had heard a lot about the strict discipline at this school—and besides I didn't know anyone. Gradually, though, I made new friends—the same kinds of friends I had had before.

For awhile I played a trumpet in a rock band. I also worked at some other part-time jobs, but most of my time was squandered on girls—one girl in particular—and parties. Mom must have known, but if so, she bore the sorrow in silent suffering.

All teen-agers will experiment. How much they experiment and how far they go depends a lot on the foundation they've been given at home and the friends they run around with. Because of the friends I had, I "played around" much more than I would have alone. I knew Mom would be hurt if she knew about my misdeeds, but I figured it wouldn't be too bad if I could just keep her from knowing, and supply her with some money now and then.

I was "manly" enough to try anything. All of us—the whole gang—pressured each other into doing things we didn't really want to do. I knew that what we were doing was wrong, but I had the choice of losing my only friends or doing the things that were suggested.

As I look back, I am ashamed of myself for allowing others—especially girls—to have so much influence over me. The pressure from girls was always more challenging than the pressure from guys. If the girl was cute enough, I always accepted the challenge.

When I was sixteen, I began making serious decisions about life and doing serious things with Joann. Joann's family situation was similar to mine. Both of us were so desperate for affection and attention that we fell into a whole series of deplorable activities. Those activities continued for years.

Joann and I had met years before when we were in eighth grade. Although she had lived in Bismarck, she had often come to Strasburg to stay with her grandparents. My grandparents lived across from hers, and it was easy to get acquainted. Both of our fathers were alcoholics, and both of them were finally commited to hospitals for extended treatment. When Joann would go back to Bismarck, we would correspond frequently and share our feelings through frequent letters. We also managed to see each other occasionally between other guys and girls.

By the time we were seniors in high school, I was convinced that we were eternally in love—which, I thought, gave us the right to live it up even more. It's very easy to rationalize the use of drugs, stealing, and premarital sex when everything else in life is out of kilter. Even though we knew it was wrong, Joann and I soon became caught in repeated acts of immorality. We did things that were wrong—things we didn't really want to do—and those things progressively became the reason for our relationship. But after a couple of years, I realized that we were using each other more than we were loving each other.

On occasion, we tried to break out of the cycle. Several times we went to confession together on a Saturday night—only to sin again later that same evening.

We didn't realize at the time that we were trapped by something much greater than ourselves—that we were being manipulated by "someone" who wanted us destroyed. We were much like some alcoholics and drug addicts: we didn't realize that we were "killing ourselves."

How were we to understand the spiritual implications of all that we were doing? The only truth we had was the doctrinal "truth" that was given to us in the classrooms of our parochial high school. Never were we challenged to find out the truth for ourselves. All we knew about God was given to us second-hand. The religion teacher would funnel the religious gobbledygook into our heads. None of it seemed to relate to my personal problems—my situation at home,

my feelings about my girl, my father's health—
or to life in general. So far as I was concerned,
religion didn't mix with anything. It was OK inside the church or classroom. Beyond that, it
had no meaning for me.

I'm convinced that many of my teachers felt
the same way. They never said it out loud like
we did, but their lives showed it.

We heard much preaching, but saw little
Christianity in action. When we "lipped off" to
our parents about some of the things that were
happening in our parochial school, they hushed
us as if we were blaspheming God.

I wondered how long it would be before the
truth about the emptiness of our "Christian education" would be discovered.

Chapter 3

*Nothing deserves to be despised more
than vice; yet I gave in more and more
to vice simply in order not to
be despised. If I had not sinned
enough to rival other sinners,
I used to pretend that I had done things
I had not done at all, because
I was afraid that innocence would
be taken for cowardice and
chastity for weakness.*

—From St. Augustine's *Confessions*
translated by R.F. Pine-Coffin
by arrangement with Penguin Books, Ltd.

B.M.O.C.?

At home, things were not getting any better. Dad had been released from the hospital supposedly cured, and had found us in Bismarck. Reluctantly, Mom decided to try making a go of it again. But it soon became apparent that the drying-out treatment had only made him more thirsty. He was soon back on the bottle, and he and Mom were again fighting like pros. I was glad when I was graduated from high school and was free to get involved in college life.

With the income from a part-time job and the rock band, I managed to finish two years at Bismarck Junior College. When I graduated, I accepted the offer of a substantial public relations scholarship to attend the University of North Dakota in Grand Forks.

I enrolled in the University in 1965, just when college campuses were becoming activistic. SDS (a left-wing organization misnamed *Students for*

37

a Democratic Society) was influential, and students were becoming more involved politically. Strikes, pickets, and rallies protesting the war in Vietnam were frequent. The campus was saturated by draft-dodging counselors, voter registration movements, and meetings sponsored by the Gay Liberation and Women's Liberation Movements. Dope-pushers were also much in evidence.

Every college campus has its own unique atmosphere. New students unconsciously absorb that atmosphere and soon find themselves doing the things that are expected of them by fellow students, teachers, fraternities, and other campus organizations. Within a short time, I too was becoming a "typical," UND student. As much as I hated having others "mold" me into a pattern, the pressure to conform was too strong and too insidious to be resisted.

In my opinion, the atmosphere of private, prestigious, denominational colleges is not immune to the pollution I am talking about. Many of these private institutions have no more of a Christian atmosphere than Caesar's Palace in Las Vegas, and the theology they teach in their required courses on religion is empty, powerless, unbiblical, and unreal.

It didn't take me long to become a B.M.O.C. (Big Man on Campus). In no time I got to know the ropes, the right people, and the lingo that it takes to make the important committees and organizations.

On most campuses, a student gets the recognition he needs from various members of the college community. From teachers, he gets recognition for his performance in class and extracurricular activities; from girls, for his manliness; from buddies, for his capacity to consume beer and drugs. I tried getting recognition in all three areas—and I am ashamed to say that I succeeded in all of them.

Seldom did I do any reflective thinking; when I did, I got nervous. One of the thoughts that made me most nervous was a simple question: "Why are you in college?" Although I knew I wanted a career in the field of advertising, I had no idea what I personally wanted out of life. So my answers to the question were all pragmatic: I went to college because I had a scholarship, I wanted a degree, and I wanted to earn lots of money. In the meantime, I wanted to have all the fun I could. Since you only live once, you need to take all you can. I took all I could from college.

In addition to holding several major positions on campus committees, I had two campus jobs—both related to advertising. They were a snap for me and they gave me almost enough money to pay my way through college. I was proud that I could be self-sufficient even in college.

But the campus involvement, the jobs, and all of the partying caught up with me. At the age of nineteen, I began to have stomach trouble—an ulcer that was to bother me for years to come. The medication prescribed for that condition, together with the large quantities of beer I drank, kept me on a perpetual high. For about two years I floated just a few feet off the ground at all times. For some reason I liked being flighty, "spacey," incoherent. Being freaky was the in thing, and my need to be accepted by everyone was so great that I thought I had to be freaky. In the meantime, I was developing a serious dependency on drugs.

It was somewhat frustrating not to be able to remember all those "good times" I had at parties. The next day, I had to ask my buddies what preposterous things I had done the night before. But that's what college life was all about: "Have another beer."

Of the many college activities I was involved in, the most meaningful were my memberships in the Sigma Chi Social Fraternity, the Blue Key Honorary Fraternity and my participation in activities related to journalism. I deliberately looked for ways to cram my schedule so that I'd never have to stop to answer that persistent question, "Why am I here?"

In my junior year I met Bart. He was working with a Christian Campus Movement, and for days he spent most waking moments with me. Finally I sat down and listened to his story, just to get rid of him. That was the first time I had heard the Christian message on a one-to-one basis, and I found it fascinating. But it wasn't for me. I admired Bart's persistence, but I disliked his message. I called him a fanatic, a Communist, a freak, a parasite, a misplaced college grad—anything but a Christian, probably because I didn't want him to get through to me. By putting labels on people, I could keep them at a distance. I didn't have to listen to what they had to say, because my mind was made up before they said it. But no matter what I thought of Bart, his message did some weird things to me.

For one thing, I felt a sense of guilt whenever I talked to Bart or any of his friends. Their very presence made me aware of sins I was too cowardly to face. Something else about those guys bothered me too. They seemed to know that my life was empty, and that I was desperately filling the emptiness with artificial things. They surmised that "good times" at parties weren't really good times at all.

In my senior year at UND, I shared a grubby three-room apartment with a guy named Ted. Ted had transferred from North Dakota State

University in Fargo. He and I had been friends in high school, and had become very close when his mother died of cancer. Ted was seventeen—and from then on we shared almost every part of our lives with each other.

We dabbled in almost every sect and organization we could find. For some time, we hung out with the philosophical gang. Later on, political activism excited us. We did a short stint with the "studs" (playboys), and occasionally turned to dope. At times we dabbled in Eastern religions and other forms of spiritual crud.

The group that was most appealing to me, though, was the "get-rich-quick crowd." It was no formal organization—just a bunch of cool, studly, "suave and debonair" guys planning to make it big some day soon.

In almost all these groups, the basic principle of life was "Don't commit yourself to anything." The attitude of most kids in college was nihilistic and hedonistic. We said, "You have only one chance in life to be completely irresponsible—and this is it!" The slogan that was most popular in our fraternity—"Whatever you do, don't face reality"—was beginning to get under my skin. With all the boozing and doping we "cool guys" were doing, I knew that it was more than a joke. For me, the flight from reality was becoming a way of life. I had become intoxicated with the desire to fulfill all of my worldly passions—every one of them. I didn't know that the fulfillment of these desires would leave ineradicable scars.

It took me a long time to realize that worldly passions are insatiable—never fully satisfied—and that they would rule me if I let them. I didn't like being controlled by something beyond me. I detested having to drink so that I could have a good time. I was getting fed up with overdoing prescribed drugs.

I had heard some campus arguments about God and Who He is, but they were only empty words. They lacked convincing power and supportive action. Most of the Christians I had met (except for Bart) couldn't clearly articulate what their faith meant to them. Their ideas were all second-hand, given them by someone else. For that reason, I questioned the sincerity of their beliefs. They were "let's-pretend" Christians, with little depth of faith. I wanted to meet a man who could speak from authority. But then it occurred to me that I had already met such a man. His name was Bart.

It was about two o'clock one morning, at the end of an evening of drinking with my buddies, that I suddenly *knew* something very significant was happening. I was beginning to ask the right questions: "Who is God really? Does He care about me? How can a guy get to know Him? What does He expect from me?"

A few weeks later I came home around four in the morning to the apartment that Ted and I shared. I had just taken my date home, and I was loaded. Ted and his "guest" for the evening were lying on the sofa. As I shuffled through the apartment door on that frigid winter night, Ted looked up and asked me why I looked so depressed.

Suddenly I realized that I was depressed and had been depressed for months—maybe years. What was more, I was fed up with the way I felt and the way I lived. "Ted," I replied, "I'm tired of living this way. I'm sick of all these 'good times.' I'm really not happy. I'm just a phony trying to convince you and everyone else that I'm happy. I'm not. I hate this way of life. I'm sick of booze, drugs, women, and parties. This irresponsible living is a bunch of crap. I can't take it any more. I can't take it!"

A short time later I dozed off to sleep with those words ringing in my ears: "I can't take it any more." But I held on till morning. When the gray day dawned and the alarm went off, I told myself—as I had many times before—"There must be more to life than this." Standing in the shower, waiting for the sharp sting of the water to clear my hungover head, I realized that I was in sad shape. Physically, spiritually, and emotionally I was a mess.

Right after Ted and I graduated from college

in 1968, he began talking about spending some time in Europe. It was one of his life's dreams. In his usual manipulative manner, he managed to convince me that I needed to take a break after graduation and before I began working. It didn't take much persuasion to get me to accompany him on a thirty-day trek through Europe. Mom and Dad had finally divorced, and I didn't feel like going back home. Subconsciously, I was hoping—and half-fearing—to find God in Europe.

We had many stimulating experiences—all of them instigated by us. I got the taste of Europe that I wanted, and a taste of something else that I didn't want—at least not consciously.

On a shivery February morning, in a shabby Left-Bank hotel in Paris, I was awakened by the happy sound of a man singing about God as he walked down the alley-way outside our room. I remembered that it was Sunday and that I hadn't been to church in a long time. I shook Ted awake and suggested that we try to make it to an early morning service. Surprisingly, he agreed. Like most American tourists, we went to the Notre Dame Cathedral. As we entered the stately, chilly structure, we saw hundreds of older people (few young Europeans go to church) gathered near the majestic altar at the front of the cathedral. We had arrived late, but we were just in time for the sermon.

The elderly, graying priest was preaching with great feeling. He walked as he spoke, and it was obvious that he was pleading with the people.

I had never studied French and could understand almost nothing of the sermon. But this man was reaching me. He was communicating with me. I kept hearing "Jesus Christ . . . Jesus Christ . . . Jesus Christ." This was the first preacher I had ever heard who spoke that name as if he really knew the One he was talking about—as if he had met this Jesus face to face.

I left Notre Dame knowing that something had touched me. But it was nothing a little Scotch couldn't drown. (Scotch was always helpful when my conscience started acting up.)

A few days later, however, as we left Paris on our return flight to the States, that man's message kept rolling around in my head. I heard his words. I felt his feelings. When I closed my eyes as we passed over the scenic French Alps, I saw his piercing, tear-filled eyes. They forced a long-suppressed question to the surface: "Ron, what do you really believe in?"

I still didn't know the answer.

Chapter 4

Give a man
a purpose in life and
he will endure
everything;
take away a man's
purpose in
life, and
he will endure nothing.

Bishop Fulton J. Sheen

In Pursuit of Success

All my life, the advertising business had fascinated me. The glamorous television commercials, the creative sounds of radio, the colorful newspaper ads—all of these had captivated me since childhood. Having worked as the manager of the student newspaper during my college days, I had developed a close relationship with the owner of an advertising agency. That friendship paid off; before I graduated, he offered me a job, and I accepted with enthusiasm. After six months' training, I opened a partnership branch office in Bismarck, and became a proud, successful ad man.

It really was success, not failure, that motivated my deeper search for God. My success in my job only seemed to accentuate the lack of success and satisfaction in my personal life. Even though I was getting citations and "outstanding achievement" awards, I lived in a state of discontent. The needs I had squelched in grade school, high school, and college were showing their miserable faces again. My questions, doubts, hurts, experiences, and sins were demanding to be dealt with.

One question in particular haunted me day and night: "What is success?" I asked myself that question repeatedly. I had seen and met hundreds of "successful" men who were still restless and discontented. What kind of success was that?

"So what if you make thousands?" I asked myself. "What will that do to solve your problems and the problems of the world? What are you doing that helps anybody else? Are you really happy? When will you quit playing the 'success game'? What about God? Heaven? Hell? Sin? Death? Your future?" These and hundreds of similar questions ganged up on me. They were like voices inside me—harassing me, defying me, stumping me—forcing me to face reality.

Up to this point, the little happiness I had known in life revolved around my work, sex, dope, drinking, money and other material things. Never did it cross my mind that I could find happiness in a less complicated way.

I knew that most of the things I was doing were wrong. There was no doubt in my mind. I knew that there had to be more to life and I wanted to get in on it, but I didn't know how.

Things were lousy. I wanted to change. Desperately, I wanted to be different. I tried everything I knew. I went on several personal improvement kicks, when I'd listen to tapes and records and follow television programs that seemed to point out avenues for self-change. I got into "positive thinking" programs, self-evaluation programs, discussions, reading, meditation. I listed my positive and negative characteristics. I even went so far as to go to church.

Even though there was nothing wrong with any of these approaches, they could not get the job done for me. Each of them touched only on one part of my life. They made me more aware of my personal weaknesses, but could not give me the power to change.

I needed something that would change every facet of my life—something that would get to the heart of my problem and change me from the inside. It seemed to me that my problem was centered around what I did. Actually, it was centered around who I was and my attitude about who I was.

Although I mused about God occasionally, I didn't see much hope in "putting any stock in His game." All my life, I had wanted something real to believe in—something I could put my whole self into, something so genuine that it could penetrate my whole being and soak up every part of me. But God didn't seem to be that "something."

As usual, I was hung up on performance. "What could I, such a cardinal sinner, ever *do* to get on God's side—to impress Him?" (I had become so accustomed to impressing others, I was convinced I would have to do the same with Him.) When I went to church, however, I didn't hear any answers to my questions. Maybe I wasn't listening. Perhaps my clouded mind couldn't comprehend all the theological jargon. Whatever the reason, I wasn't getting what I needed.

I turned more and more to drinking, partying, and carousing as a means of escape. "Scotch on the rocks"—it's amazing how many "exciting" discussions were stimulated by the stuff, and how my life was controlled by it. I rationalized that it was good to drink so much. I drank so that I could work better—and worked so that I could drink more. "All things work together for good. . . ." (KJV). (I knew that was from the Bible, but I hadn't bothered to learn the whole of Romans 8:28.)

I was always impatiently fretting to move on to some different place, some new experience, some other party. I was never content to be where I was. Happiness and contentment were always somewhere "out there"—in some elusive future or some distant place. My nights were sleepless and my days filled with hectic activity.

At times I would recall the "good ol' days," letting my mind dwell on the relationships I had had with many girls during my high school and college years. One by one, they would come into mind. The memories were so intense that I experienced all over again what I had experienced with each one of them, what it was like afterwards, and how I felt when they were no longer with me.

That's when the guilt feelings began to overwhelm me—when I was alone after one of those memory sessions. The drinking, the illicit sex, and all the other sins I had not faced or dealt with came before me. One sin stacked upon another—like wormy pancakes—a mile high. The cumulative guilt was more than I could bear. I hated being alone at such times, and I would become almost frantic with the desire to go somewhere and talk to someone who could comfort me.

Granted, these guilt spells were few and far between. My conscience was so calloused that very little affected it any more. But when these spells did come, the thought of suicide was not far off. The more clearly I saw my sins, the more I hated myself. I hated what I had done to others and what I was doing to myself. And yet I kept right on sinning. The more I tried to quit, the more impossible it seemed.

When I jokingly mentioned the subject of guilt in conversation with other people, I knew that they too were experiencing it to some degree. I found that each man has his own way of dealing with it. Some escape it with drugs; some drown it in alcohol; some avoid it by filling their time with worries, television, entertainment, hobbies, busy schedules, or other avoidance mechanisms. None of these worked for me.

I was unwilling to face myself completely, for fear of what I might find. But somehow, I had to discover some way to deal with all this crud in my system.

Much as I needed to escape from myself and my guilt, the "leap of faith" had no appeal for me; I was afraid I might have to give up my "goodies." When I reflected on what those goodies really were, I realized that they were only meaningless material things and pleasures. But they were all that I had. I knew of nothing that could replace them except faith—and that was too chancy for me.

Over and over, like a treadmill, the same question and the same answer kept running through my mind:

"What's causing all this guilt?"

"Sin."

"What's causing all this guilt?"

"Sin."

I recognized now that I had been a sinner

from my very early years, and that I was becoming worse. To the sins of drinking and fornication, I had added profession-oriented sins such as lying and cheating in business. But the most devastating sins were those of the spirit—especially pride. Pride kept me believing in my own ability to do anything I made up my mind to do. Because of pride, I was unwilling to have anyone else (even God) interfere with my life, much less run it.

Finally I came to the realization that my greatest source of guilt was my complete neglect of, hatred for, and separation from God. Through guilt, He made me see how much I needed Him.

But when I considered turning to God, fear of losing my friends held me back—even though when I asked myself if they really *were* friends, I knew the answer was negative. All I had in common with these "friends" was Joseph Schlitz, Scotch, drugs, parties, and "good times." When I occasionally voiced my despair to them, they couldn't help. They too were in search of something real.

One morning in the office, I read a magazine article about an ad man who had experienced much of what I was going through. This man's life had been changed so dramatically that he was now working as an artist for a Christian group. The article impressed me, especially since it appeared in the "Bible" of the advertising business: *Advertising Age.* I wondered if anything like that could ever happen to me.

The next day I casually mentioned the article to a client who happened to be in my office, and asked him what he thought. He became excited. Obviously, religion was his favorite subject. It was a hot summer day and my stuffy little office was unbearable. But this man didn't let discomfort deter him. He began to probe into my spiritual state. "Ron," he finally said, "you look troubled. Are you happy?"

"Of course," I responded glibly.

After several other embarrassing questions, he finally asked, "Do you know Jesus Christ?"

"I go to church," was my reply.

He said, "I didn't ask you that. I asked you if you knew Jesus."

"I've just returned from a weekend retreat."

"I didn't ask you *that.* I asked you if you knew Jesus Christ."

Knowing that I was trapped, I responded honestly, "Maybe I do and maybe I don't. Can you ever be sure?"

He said, "Of course," and then pulled out Billy Graham's "Four Steps to Peace" and proceeded to read it to me. Because he was a new client, I listened politely, tolerating what I considered to be pure gibberish. It was with relief that I finally dismissed him from my office. I wrote him off as a fanatic and thought that was the end of the matter.

A few days later, I picked up Michel Quoist's book, *The Meaning of Success*. The title intrigued me, and for the next couple of days I spent my lunch hours and evenings reading it. As I did so, a new definition of success began to emerge for me. The book made me aware for the first time that there are some occupations in which it is impossible for a man to live a "successful" Christian life. When a man discovers that he is in such an occupation, and when God speaks to him about changing his job, that man must obediently respond by getting out. Strangely enough, I felt a tugging to get out of the advertising field.

Chapter 5

We are going to have a feast,
a celebration,
because this son of mine
was dead and has come
back to life;
he was lost and is found.

Luke 15: 23, 24

Tug-of-War Ended

Bart, magazine articles, television programs, books, Billy Graham, and the client in my office: all of them were repeating the same thing. Their consistency really impressed me. I knew there had to be some truth in what they said but I was afraid to face it.

Mom had taught me as a child, however, that a man must face his worst fear, whatever it is, before he can move on in life. He must confront it and conquer it before it warps him permanently. Scared as I was, I knew I couldn't put off facing this one.

Because of my pride and tremendous desire for independence, the idea of "surrendering myself to God" was extremely difficult for me to accept. But the time came when I knew this issue had to be settled once and for all.

I was alone in a plush bachelor apartment in Bismarck—an apartment I shared with a friend.

The thickly carpeted living room was dark. I was the subject of a tug-of-war between two opposing forces. The argument went something like this:

"You must receive Me personally. You must surrender everything to Me."

"No, everything is OK. You're just dreaming these things. You're a good person. You go to church. You love people."

"But that's not enough, Ron. I love you, and I need you to love Me. Come to Me. Come to Me."

"Everything is OK. You don't want to be fanatical about this, do you? Everything is OK. Everything is OK."

This verbal battle went on for more than three hours while I sweat, trembled, and agonized over the decision that had to be made. I knew that something very, very real was happening and that I had to make up my mind about "which side I wanted to join." With weak knees and a heavy heart, I walked to my bedroom and knelt by the bed. For the first time in my life, I prayed to Jesus—a prayer that came directly from my heart.

"Jesus," I said, "I don't know You. I am convinced that I have done a lot of things wrong. My life is a mess. I've heard that You can do something about it. If you can, I give it all to

You right now. Make me what You want me to be. Help me to know You. I need You."

Jesus answered my prayer. He came into my life. He was *real.* He loved me and I was experiencing His wonderful love right there in my own bedroom. I was so overwhelmed with the flood of His love that I wept—tears of shame, tears of relief, tears of gratitude and joy.

The conflict that I had been dodging for so many years—finally, it was all settled. God was real and I had chosen to be on His side. After all the things I had tried to do to change myself, this encounter with Jesus Christ had made me into a new person.

In my search for meaning and reality—which I now knew was a search for God—I had failed to take into consideration the fact that He too was searching for me. I didn't have to *win* His friendship; He *gave* it to me. All I had to do was ask for it.

As I look back on this experience and the many others that led to it and followed it, I realize that there is a sense in which conversion is a process. First my intellect had given assent; now my will had surrendered; but only over a period of time and in a series of stages would my emotions and the rest of my being come into line.

I don't believe I was a Christian before the surrender of my will. My decision to accept

Jesus as my personal Lord and Savior was the key experience in the whole process.

Now that I had settled, once and for all, the question of whose side I was on, Christ became a reality to me and I knew that I was free—free from myself, my past sins, and my undisciplined way of life. I was certain of my destiny—and when a man knows his destiny, his whole life style changes. I was aware of the supporting presence of the Holy Spirit and of His help in reading and understanding the Bible. Gradually, my language was cleaned up, my drinking decreased, and my nerves began to settle down.

One of the reasons I had put off accepting Christ was the fear of forfeiting my unique self-identity and personality. I was scared of becoming one of those pious, somber, narrow-minded, legalistic Christians I had been exposed to. Now I was learning that only Jesus can free me to be completely myself, without fear of what others think or say. Without Him, I have no identity at all.

At the same time, I became aware of new dimensions in life. I developed a new taste for good music. I loved being alone—I who had always craved companionship twenty-four hours a day! I began to appreciate the simple things in life: flowers, birds, grass, sunsets, rain, walks in the forest. These and other ordinary miracles began to intrigue me.

All the truth that I had sought in hundreds of books, relationships and conversations, I found in a Person—a living, loving God, revealed in Jesus Christ.

I praise God that His answer is so simple, and that His unique cure for thousands upon thousands of sins is permanent and eternal. I praise God that His answer is personal: Himself.

But I'm getting ahead of my story. Many of these developments took place weeks or months after that evening I surrendered my will to Jesus and found Him to be real.

When my roommate came home later that night, he looked at me as if he had found a stranger in his apartment. I didn't even try to tell him what had happened to me.

"Ron," he smiled solicitously, "do you want a Scotch?"

"No, thanks," I replied. "Not *now*."

Chapter 6

Jesus said,
"If you wish to be perfect, go
and sell what you own and
give the money to the poor,
and you will
have treasure in heaven;
then come, follow me."

Matthew 19:21

The Bleak Room on Third Floor

Everything was different after I yielded to Christ. Now, more than ever, I knew there'd have to be some changes in the ad business. Either I'd have to make some radical modifications, or get out altogether.

I decided to try the former first. John, my partner, had come up from Norfolk, Virginia, to join me a few months before my conversion. I'd heard about him through correspondence with some friends, and it was a seemingly successful merger right from the start. We were shaking the money-tree hard.

But now I began to re-assess what we were doing. I could no longer be satisfied with merely making money. There had to be a better reason for our business than that. We had to do something constructive to minister to the needs of people. Otherwise, what would I do with all these challenging ideas I was becoming aware of?

I knew I had to play it cool around John though. Without saying anything to him about my new desires for our business, I began to look for some new clients. Soon we were doing work for some mental health organizations, and other groups that were serving the needs of people. The more of this kind of work we did, the better I felt.

It wasn't long until John noticed that about half of our work had become public service! But public service always ends in one's asking himself whether he shouldn't do more of it. It became increasingly clear to me that God was summoning me to leave the advertising world. But where was I to go from there? Having no idea, I waited for God to show me.

During that year, my eyes were opened to the appalling needs that all people have—needs I had never noticed before. I couldn't understand why more people, especially Christians, weren't doing anything to meet those needs. Remembering my own unhappy adolescence, I was particularly concerned about teen-agers and their need for a friend.

About that time, a priest asked me to teach an after-school class in Christian doctrine for some of the parish kids. It was through this class that I began to see the pathetic needs of teen-agers, and started to wonder what I could do to help them

There was one boy in particular who intrigued me, and I made a point to set up a time to rap with him.

We met in a pizza joint. We talked for awhile about some of the problems other kids were having. Finally, in a challenging, bitter tone of voice, he said, "And you—what are *you* doing about all these hurting people? Why the hell don't *you* do something about them?" His question hit me hard. It was almost as though God had spoken through that boy.

That question followed me around for days. It caused violent turmoil within me. I knew I had to face the question, and face it head on. It was another crisis-creating question.

Finally, I took a few days off from the office and ended up in a small-town motel. I walked into the room—a room without a TV, phone, or radio—and set down my box of books and my Bible. "Lord," I said, "I need to know what You are asking me to do. I'm going to stay here alone until You reveal to me very clearly what You have in mind."

When I checked out of that resort motel three days later, I knew that I had to give up the advertising business and enter a seminary. I knew also how my partner, my parents, and my friends would react to that decision, and how hard it would be to make the necessary arrangements. But the inner peace that I experienced as I did what God had commanded transcended any earthly trials.

Several businessmen I had been close to arranged a farewell party in my honor. It was a heartwarming gesture, because I loved these men and their associates. But it was an awkward, embarrassing experience. All my "old buddies" were there to give testimonies about my accomplishments personally and as an ad man. But most of them didn't know what to make of my far-out decision, and they were as standoffish as if I had suddenly developed leprosy. In the back of their minds, they were wondering, "Where did this guy go wrong?" In their shoes, I guess I would have wondered the same thing.

My arrangements to enter St. John's Seminary at Collegeville, Minnesota, were finally completed in January of 1970. Realizing I could take only a few of my belongings with me, I sold some and gave others away. Parting with my material possessions and my friends wasn't nearly as hard as giving up my worldly security—the successful business I had worked so hard to create. But I had learned that security comes from God—not from salaries, insurances, fringe benefits, and material goods.

I decided to ask my father to give me a ride to the seminary. Since he and Mom had split up, he had been living alone in an apartment in Bismarck. I knew he'd jump at the opportunity. Underneath it all, he had always wanted to help. I had often talked with Mom about my new relationship with Christ, but not Dad. He still had his drinking problem, and God only knows how I wanted to help him! I was hoping the trip would give me a chance to share with him my joy in following Christ.

But it didn't work that way. As he looked at me through the blue haze of his cigarette smoke, all he saw was a crackpot son who had gone off the deep end. His face was drawn and too serious. I tried to explain to him that this was what God was asking me to do—but he still thought I had blown my head on some drug or something. Our eight-hour drive was made in heavy silence.

When we finally arrived at the seminary, Dad and I walked into the drab stone building where I was to be housed, trying to hush the echo of our too-loud footsteps. It was much like an ancient castle: gloomy and dark, with stained-glass windows. Pictures of pious saints were hung all around the entrance hall.

Although our footsteps echoed loudly on the brick floor, no one appeared to offer assistance. We stood around for about twenty minutes before a young seminarian came in and asked if he could be of help.

"Any rooms here?" I asked.

"One on the third floor," he replied. "Follow me."

As we carried our belongings up the uneven stone stairs, I began to doubt my own sanity. When he opened the door to my room, I knew I had flipped my lid. The contrast between the luxurious bachelor pad I had vacated earlier that day and the bleak room that I was gazing into seemed more than I could endure.

After we unloaded my few belongings, I walked with my father to the car. He asked me to get in with him.

"Ron," he said after lighting a fresh cigarette, "I don't think you will be here long—I don't think this place is for you. You can still change your mind and ride back with me. Do you wanna do it?"

I glanced at his saddened face, and thought I saw his lip quiver. Did I wanna do it? At that moment, nothing could have been more appealing. But I couldn't back out now.

"Dad, I'll make it," I said. "I know I'm doing the right thing."

I looked over to see my father's eyes brimming with tears. It was the first time I had ever seen him cry, and it hurt me. Underneath the facade, Dad had so many beautiful qualities and feelings.

"You'll need a car here," he said after a long silence. "I'll buy you a car and let you know when I have it." I knew that was his way of telling me he loved me and cared about me. Dad had always found it hard to express love. But when he gave a gift, we knew what he meant.

"I'd appreciate that," I replied as I got out of his car. "Just let me know." As he drove off into the sunset, I wished I had been able to hug him and tell him how much he meant to me. I did want to go with him and he knew it.

I went back up to my drab room to unpack my things. It must have been three or four hours before I saw another face. During that time, I struggled with mixed feelings of dismay and joy, frustration and contentment.

Before retiring, I knelt beside the bed. Looking at a crucifix hanging on the wall, I said, "Jesus, I am all Yours. I am here. Please help me."

After I crawled into bed, I began to cry. For several nights I fell asleep thinking, "I've made a mistake. I've blown my cool. I'm really a fanatic." But a quieter and mightier voice repeated its comforting message time and time again: "I love you. You are Mine. Please rest."

That voice convinced me that things would get better, that there was a design in my being there. As I began to study, read, and pray, I watched the plan unfold.

Chapter 7

Now this Lord is
the Spirit, and
where the Spirit of the Lord is,
there is freedom.

2 Corinthians 3:17

Unfinished Business

The first few weeks of my seminary life were spent largely in depression and figuring out where I went wrong. But after I got through the Slough of Despond, I perked up a little and began looking for Christian fellowship. The word soon got out that I was something of a "fanatic." That was when I decided that one of my tasks in seminary was to share my experience with the many students who apparently didn't know God.

To this end, I began taking part in late-evening bull sessions as often as I could. In many of these, the main topic of discussion was God's power. The more I studied the Bible, the more I noticed the passages that dealt with this subject.

I began an intense search for the truth about God's work in the world today. The more I studied and questioned, the more clearly I saw that I needed more than just a salvation experience. I needed power to put skin on my experience and live it out consistently. Though I was still happy about my new life in Christ, I was encountering some difficulties—difficulties with praying, with understanding the Bible, with living a victorious life, and with serving others.

Larry, a fellow student from Texas, gave me three books that really piqued my interest: *The Cross and the Switchblade* by David Wilkerson, *Speaking in Tongues* by Larry Christenson, and *Aglow with the Spirit* by Robert Frost. These books and many discussions with Larry made me acutely aware of the need for a deeper relationship with God. My heart longed to be closer to Him, to know Him more intimately.

After much persistence, Larry finally prevailed upon me to attend one of those "wild charismatic prayer meetings" that were beginning to pop up like posies all over the Midwest. I went—and never before had I been so turned off. I left that meeting feeling like I had been to a freak show. If that was what Larry meant by a "deeper walk with the Lord," he could forget it as far as I was concerned. I wanted nothing to do with those "weirdos."

Setting the whole idea aside, I tried to settle back and enjoy what I already had in Christ. But God didn't want me to become stagnant. A few weeks later, He showed me that I had blocked Him and His Spirit by my conditioned reactions to what others said and did. Like many another sincere Christian, I had turned my back on a real experience of God because someone's expression of that experience didn't appeal to my sense of propriety.

As I read and prayed, God challenged me to keep investigating the matter. I told him that if He wanted me to, He would have to revive my dying interest.

He granted my request by permitting me to get into a spiritual slump—an experience that is not unusual to relatively new Christians. For weeks I was unable to feel His presence and, like most Christians, I panicked and became afraid that He might have left me. I cried out to God for help—for some assurance of His reality and His presence with me.

Returning to my room late one evening, I picked up *Aglow with the Spirit* and began to read in the fourth chapter. Although my attitude was skeptical, each page of chapters 4, 5, and 6 convinced me of my need for a more dynamic Christian experience.

I had previously been convinced that what happened to the apostles at Pentecost was a once-and-for-all event—like the crucifixion. But as I followed Dr. Frost's logic and read the scripture verses that he quoted, I became certain that the Pentecostal experience is for *all* believers, and I *knew* that I needed this experience.

I had been a Christian long enough to know that spiritual experiences can take place only where there is faith—willingness to step out with an expectant attitude. But what step was I to take? I had salvation. I knew Christ. But I also knew that parts of my life were still not "right with God."

Again I sought out Larry and shared my feelings with him. I was relieved when he told me he had gone through the same thing. Then he asked me if I was willing to have him pray with me, using what he called a "traditional church gesture." Not knowing what the traditional gesture was going to be, I was a little hesitant to go along with him—but finally I submitted.

As he prayed, my fears were relieved by his earnest and loving supplications for me. Even more heartwarming was the "gesture."

Gently placing his hands on my head, he asked God to bless me, quiet me, and teach me what He wanted me to know. Although nothing exceptional happened at the time, I felt that God was dealing with me in a new and exciting way.

Alone in my room later, I opened the Bible to study again those passages that deal with the Holy Spirit. Turning to the book of Acts, I read the first seven verses of chapter 19. My special concern was with verse 2: "Did you receive the Holy Spirit when you became believers?"

I was not sure that I had received the Holy Spirit. I knew the arguments of those who say that you receive it automatically when you accept Jesus Christ—but I was bothered by my own uncertainty. (To me, the Spirit was always an "*it*"—a formula, a doctrine, a "ghost." I had never known Him as a person.)

Then I read Mark 1:1-8. The eighth verse—"I have baptized you with water, but He will baptize you with the Holy Spirit"—disturbed me. I knew I had been baptized with water; but what was the baptism in the Holy Spirit? Was it a special, separate experience?

Then I read John 14: 15-16 and asked, "Who is this *Advocate*—this *Spirit of truth*? Do I know Him?" Even though the answer seemed to be negative, I was comforted by the promise in Luke 11:13: "How much more will the heavenly Father give the Holy Spirit to those who ask Him!"

It began to make sense. I had never asked the Father for the Spirit. Perhaps that was why I didn't know for sure that He was dwelling in me.

I was puzzled by Luke 24:49. What did Jesus mean when He told the disciples, just before His ascension, to "stay in the city then, until you are clothed with the power from on high"? He spoke of that power as "what the Father has promised." Then why hadn't I experienced it?

Turning once more to Acts, I read the first eleven verses of chapter 1 and all of chapter 2. Verse 39 convinced me that the promise and experience of baptism in the Holy Spirit are for men in all ages—not just for those in the upper room at Pentecost. I turned back to the Gospel of John and read in the seventh chapter (verses 37-39) the promise of Jesus that those who believed on Him would receive the Spirit and that streams of living water would flow from them. In chapter 20 (verse 22) I read how He had breathed on the disciples, *commanding* them to receive the Holy Spirit. Quietly, I asked God to show me the whole truth about this matter.

The next day, I spoke with several others who had had the charismatic experience and whose lives were a living witness to the fact that something extraordinary had happened to them. They gave me even more Scripture passages to think about.

That night I continued with my study by reading the first chapter of Ephesians. I couldn't recall having been "stamped with the seal of the Holy Spirit" (verse 13), or receiving this "pledge of our inheritance" (verse 14).

Seeking to learn more, I turned back to Acts and read the account of how others had received the Holy Spirit (Acts 8:14-17; 9:1-18; 10:44-48; 11:15-17.)

After reading 1 Corinthians 2:14-16, I begged the Holy Spirit to give me the understanding I needed. That was the first time I had addressed the Spirit directly.

Finally I was convinced. The evidence was before me. Plainly, I needed a closer walk with God, and this deeper awareness of the Spirit would seemingly give me that walk.

I closed my Bible and quietly asked Jesus to do this thing to me. "Jesus," I said, "You are the Baptizer in the Spirit. Please baptize me. Please fill me with your Spirit. I need Your Holy Spirit."

Nothing happened. After waiting for awhile, I prepared to go to bed. As usual, my last act of preparation was to kneel beside my bed, confess my sins of the day, and thank God for His forgiveness.

Then I crawled into bed and burrowed into my pillow. I was exhausted—but I couldn't sleep. I felt as though there was some unfinished business that had to be dealt with—*now*. Wearily, I climbed back out of bed and, again on my knees, asked God what He had to tell me.

As I prayed, I felt prompted to try a new form of prayer—but I wasn't sure how I should go about it. Again I asked God for help: "Lord, I'm afraid of what's happening here. Whatever it is, please speak to me clearly. I need to have things spelled out. What is it that You want to tell me?" In a few minutes, I was praying in an untried language.

I could hardly believe it was happening to me—this experience that I had heard about and had read about in the Bible. The more I prayed, the more jubilant I felt. Before long, I was deeply in love with Jesus. Never before had I felt such union with anyone. I don't know how long I stayed on my knees—perhaps an hour. I felt that I was being enveloped and absorbed by another Person.

I was so excited that I didn't want to sleep. But knowing I had to get up early, I reluctantly went to bed, still praying in my new tongue.

In that one glorious night, I was healed of things that had bothered me for years. My stomach trouble cleared up. Nervous tension abated. My hyperactive mind calmed down. My two-and-a-half-pack-a-day smoking habit began to wither away. Memories of my past hurts and past sins faded. Ill feelings toward old friends, relatives, and family members left me. I was free—free to be myself, free to love others wherever they were.

This experience gave me renewed assurance of God's love, the power to *live* what I believed and the courage to give Jesus public honor. It healed my memories and my emotions. It gave me the ability to look at all men with eyes of love. It revealed things to me in the Bible that I had never seen before, and made God's Word come *alive.*

Even though I knew this experience could never be explained by the intellect, I attempted to draw up a scriptural, concrete, factual explanation of it to help me understand it better.

I began by re-reading all the materials I had already gone over in the Bible. First Corinthians 12, 13, and 14, Romans 8 and 12, Galatians 5, and Ephesians 4 were very much alive for me. The whole book of Acts spoke directly to me as did John 14, 15 and 16.

On the very practical level, I had to find answers for my own skeptical questions about speaking in tongues: Why do I need this gift? What is it going to do for me? When can I use such a language? Where? With whom? What can I expect to happen when I use it? What is the sense in it?

First of all, I knew that my tongues experience had nothing to do with my salvation—except that it made it more vivid. Salvation had been a certainty long before that experience.

I also knew that all Christians need to be filled with the Spirit; I learned that early in my Christian life. It took me a longer time to learn that the way in which we are filled with the Spirit is different for each of us.

I also discovered to my surprise that the baptism in the Holy Spirit is very common among contemporary Christians, and that it has never died out completely since the day of Pentecost.

Most important, I learned that this experience is something that is to be specifically asked for; it doesn't just happen.

I had thought this experience was only for the Pentecostal sects—sometimes sneeringly referred to as "Holy Rollers." I had asked myself, "Who would *want* such an experience except uneducated, emotional members of the lower class?" How wrong I was! I have since spent time with men of every profession, including theologians and philosophers, who have anticipated and received this exciting experience.

I saw that the Holy Spirit had been imparted to me so that I could glorify Christ, live a victorious Christian life, and be more capable of loving others. The experience in itself was not something I should proclaim, or boast about. It was not to be an end in itself, as some well-meaning friends had led me to believe.

For me, speaking in tongues is simply one of many ways of praying. Although I don't understand the words that I find myself saying, I know they are words of worship and that I am in full control. The Holy Spirit does not force me to utter these words, but He supplies them when I choose to speak them. In most cases, the purpose of this prayer language is to build up my faith and keep me strong. It gives me immediate release from my worldly cares, and instant awareness of God's presence, and an abundance of joy and merriment. It also speaks about concerns of mine that I am not even aware of.

I reserve this prayer language almost entirely for my private prayer times. When I find my words inadequate to express my feelings of love and praise, I revert to this prayer language. It is most helpful when I am praying for others and am not sure what I should pray about.

The practice of prayer with tongues has opened the way to a more thorough understanding of the Bible and has given me a burning desire to read it.

I can use this gift while I am doing other things: shaving, driving—even while I am showering. In my experience, it has been an aid to "praying ... on every possible occasion" (Ephesians 6:18).

Through the ages, this gift has been misused, abused, misrepresented, and criticized. It would be sheer folly to attempt to combat the arguments against it. I do not need to defend a gift that has vitalized my faith, strengthened my desire to study the Bible, nurtured my daily prayer life, and given me a deep longing to seek out my hurting brothers. I do not need to justify a gift that has helped me to live out the great commands to love God and love my brother. Even if tongues is the least of the gifts, as some say, it has helped me in the area that had given me the most difficulty: loving.

But I should make it clear that the baptism in the Holy Spirit was not a cure-all for me. It did not settle all my problems. I still grappled with many of the basic principles of Christian living, and created new complications by my own foolishness.

One bit of foolishness was trying to toss out all of my previous life. I wanted to become a new man, separating myself completely from where I had been. I cut off my relationships with those who had not had my experience and decided that it was just "me and God" from here on out. I didn't realize that a man's life is a process toward wholeness—that we can never disconnect ourselves completely from our past or others.

For a time I assumed that the Holy Spirit had done away with the need for reason, logic, thought, and study. My interpretation of the promise made in John 16:13 (that "the Spirit ... will lead you to the complete truth") was that I was discharged from any responsibility to learn, to study, to struggle with intellectual questions. If I wanted to understand a Christian's responsibility toward war, I would check the Bible and pray. Unless I received a specific revelation, I assumed that I was not to get concerned about such worldly affairs.

My interpretation of Isaiah 53:5 and 1 Peter 2:24 (*"Through his wounds you have been healed"*) was that if I had a toothache, the Lord would either take away the pain or replace my tooth in some spiritually magic way. I thought dentists and doctors were only for those whose faith wasn't strong enough to allow God to heal them without human intervention.

I also believed that my baptism in the Holy Spirit had given me instant maturity in the Christian faith. Those who had had years of theological training, I felt, knew nothing at all. Theirs was a staid, powerless religion, and it was my calling (specifically mine) to be sure that they heard about the real thing.

It took me quite some time to see the mistakes I was making. Like many others, I fell victim to spiritual pride after being baptized in the Holy Spirit, and wouldn't listen to advice from any mere human. Finally, however, I realized that the Holy Spirit does not even *want* to be a substitute for our thought processes, common sense, logic, reason and study; He simply adds a new dimension to them. He compelled me to face the fact that I had not received instant maturity, knowledge, and insight. Then He showed me that, if I was willing, He would lead me into experiences through which I could grow.

My greatest challenge since my baptism in the Holy Spirit has been to keep the experience in proper perspective, and I soon found that I had to use every rational means available in order to do this. I learned that this experience was only one ingredient of life and that it had to be carefully blended with the whole batter of my life.

Many Spirit-baptized people that I have met confess that they too have to struggle constantly to stay aware of other dimensions in life: the "social gospel" (fighting war, poverty, injustice); human relationships (with family, friends, social and business acquaintances); care of the physical body (rest, recreation, and adequate attention to health); and development of the intellectual faculties through reading both spiritual and secular materials. The temptation to think of these things as "unspiritual" and therefore unworthy of our attention is a real one and a dangerous one. "Superspiritual" Christians can do more harm than good.

God wants Christians to be well balanced, so that they can bring His power to bear upon all areas of life. It hasn't been easy for me to learn this lesson, and I still have to struggle for perspective and balance.

Still, it has been worth it. I remember going

up to the barren room on the third floor one evening a few months after my baptism, and flopping down on my bed in a jubilant mood. "Lord," I laughed, "You don't know how hard it is for me to keep from being a wild fanatic about You!"

But a voice from above seemed to say, "Easy, Ron,—easy!"

Many of my friends seemed to be saying the same thing.

Chapter 8

No mere man
has ever seen, heard
or even imagined what
wonderful things
God has ready for those
who love the Lord.

1 Corinthians 2:9 (TLB)

The Too-narrow Way

"I've got to get out of here," I kept saying to myself at seminary. "I'm just wasting my time with all this academic junk."

But on the other hand there was Mom to consider. She had been so elated when I told her I was going to become a priest! Wasn't that what every Catholic mother dreamed of—to have a priest in the family?

I wrote to her and gently hinted that I wasn't sure that I really belonged at St. John's—just to see what her reaction would be. Her reply was about what I expected. She said I'd have to make my own decision—but I could read a lot of hurt between the lines. So I decided to stick it out until June.

The lifeless theology I was getting in my classes drove me more and more to extra-curricular reading, although I kept up my class studies as a matter of duty. My professors would have labeled most of my outside reading material as "charismatic junk"—but it was strange how much this "junk" blessed me!

The matter of celibacy for priests bothered me. I wasn't sure that I really wanted to spend the rest of my life single—or even if I *should*. What if I became a priest and then found someone I really wanted to marry? What would I do then? As meritorious as celibacy can be, I felt that each man should be free to choose it for himself.

And then there was my growing interest in young people. I found myself wondering how a *priest* could be especially effective in ministering to rebellious kids who'd "had it" with preachers and churches.

But the seminary days weren't altogether wasted. The semi-isolation did me good. It gave me a chance to do a lot of praying about what I was going to do with my life.

By the time June rolled around, I went back to Bismarck to live with Mom for a while—with some misgivings. I knew the subject of the priesthood was bound to come up—and I had almost made up my mind that I wouldn't be going back to seminary.

Mom was glad to see me. She'd been quite lonely and depressed since the divorce.

"Pull up a chair," she said as she flitted around the kitchen, putting the finishing touches on the meal she'd prepared. "I'll bet my young priest is famished!"

I ignored her comment and said something about being hungry as a bear. After we sat down to eat, I was careful not to get into any serious conversation about my plans. So we spent the next hour or so making small talk.

After supper, Mom said, "Ron, are you going to get a job for the summer? You'll be needing money for the fall term at the seminary, won't you?" She looked almost beautiful as she sat there beaming at me with obvious pride.

"I don't know," I replied softly. "I'm not sure about going back. As I told you before, I've been thinking about a change."

"Oh." She tried to hide her feelings, but she was visibly let down. I could imagine that she had been praying and praying that I'd change my mind.

"I'll know for sure by fall," I said. "Would it be all right for me to live with you until then?"

"I'd love that," she smiled. "In fact, I was hoping you would."

After staying with her for a few weeks, however, I decided I needed more time to myself. After looking around, I found a nice little house in the country. Mom couldn't understand why I wanted to live alone, and she made me promise to visit her often—which I did.

After landing a job as Assistant Director of

the North Dakota Catholic Conference (an arm of the Catholic Church that deals with social problems), I started making the rounds of all the prayer groups in the area. Yet I failed to find the deep, warm, honest fellowship that I needed. To a large extent, this was my own fault. In each group, I made it a point to reveal as little as possible about myself and my own personal struggles. So far as I was concerned, Christianity was strictly a personal experience between God and me.

For a while, my spiritual journey became such an intense thing that it developed into a new form of escapism, almost as abominable as some of the things I had done in my non-Christian life to avoid reality and its pains. I was so introspective, so concerned about my own spiritual growth that I was neglecting the needs of those around me. Life, real problems, the real world—all these were for the less saintly.

Whenever gusty and controversial issues—war, abortion, politics, injustice, racism, and other social concerns—were brought up, I hid behind the Bible and the cross. Rationalizing that it is God's world, not mine, I assumed little personal responsibility for its maladies. My concept of Christianity had become very narrow. Locked into a stifling, exacting theology, I was more concerned with understanding the latest theological fad than I was with the human needs that have been around for hundreds of years.

At one point in this heavy spritual journey, I was doing meditation several times during the day. Sometimes I would spend hours in contemplation. I continued that practice until I was told by a former user of LSD that I was doing something very much like the astro-projection of the mind-control cults—an exercise that separates the mind and spirit from the body.

Fall came and went, and I didn't go back to seminary. I was more concerned with sharing "sound doctrine" although it bothered me that most of the groups I visited didn't appreciate my insights into the Scriptures.

Perhaps it was just as well that I didn't find fellowship in any of the groups during this "superspiritual" phase of my life. Each one had its own interpretation of the Bible and its own peculiar emphasis.

"We have been called by Christ," one group said, "to cast out demons. That and that alone is our mission." Another group taught that it was the "one true Chruch."

I heard other far-out teachings in some of the groups I visited: That only those who spoke in tongues would be saved. That no Christian could smoke or associate with those who did. That only those who had been baptized in the Spirit would find salvation. That all Christians

101

had to be immersed in water. That if one was truly a Christian, he could not belong to *that* denomination. That those who didn't believe in the premillennial return of Christ were not Christians at all.

It may have been fortunate that, because I considered myself one of the more spiritual people around, I took little advice from others. Consequently, I didn't accept all these cramped and warped teachings that I was exposed to. This same superspiritual attitude, however, also prevented me from listening to sound advice from my more level-headed Christian friends and kept me for a long time in a spiritual maze. I knew my life was out of perspective, but I was unwilling to admit it.

During this time I too was guilty of distorting the message of Christ and the work of the Spirit. I was more concerned with some of the "deeper" dimensions of the Christian faith (demonology, fasting, meditation, prophecy, for example) than I was with the central figure of the Bible: Jesus Christ, the Messiah, Savior and Redeemer. There was a time when I knew more about demons than I did about the power and work of Christ.

Complex questions that had been the subject of intense study by hundreds of Bible scholars I shrugged off with one or two simple Bible verses. If people didn't accept my explanation, I rationalized that it was because they were not as spiritual as I was. Intelligence, I believed, had little place in one's spiritual life. In fact, there was a time when I denied the fact that I had a degree and graduate work behind me. Recognition of such vainglorious achievements was too worldly for me.

During that narrow-minded phase of my pilgrimage, I questioned the validity of any spiritual experience that wasn't just like mine. I thought everyone had to see a light, have a vision, and manifest the Spirit in the same way I did. To my own satisfaction, I had interpreted, exaggerated, and distorted many New Testament verses to support my position.

It's people like me (as I was then) who turn others away from the charismatic experience! Why would anyone want to be the way I was—obnoxious, spiritually aloof, narrow-minded? My experience had gotten me into a deep rut. It had become an end in itself—an end that I believed everyone had to achieve.

I sought to relive that experience again and again. I became preoccupied with finding new ways of rediscovering what I had already been through. I lusted after a repetition of the "good feeling"—the spine-tingling experience. Instead of moving on to the other things God had for me, I selfishly wanted to stay where I was—in my own personal, comfortable understanding of

Christianity. I felt much like Peter did at the transfiguration: I wanted to stay on the mountain with the Lord. *He* wanted me down in the valley taking care of the needs of people.

The charismatic renewal is, without a doubt, a definite answer to prayers—prayers of men who have gone before us and prayers of those who are still with us. It is the most powerful move of God that has taken place in many generations. Some of its explosive effects are being felt in churches of all demoninations across the United States and in foreign lands. Thousands of Christians have been given a miraculous infusion of power because of the charismatic experience.

Because of the temptation to overestimate and misuse this power, however, many have fallen into erroneous doctrines. No one warned me of this danger until I had swallowed some of those erroneous doctrines myself. But the charismatic renewal is so real and so vital that it can withstand the correction it needs.

I thank God for Bernie and Ken—two mature, balanced Christians who finally gave me the correction *I* needed. Bernie, the shy but affectionate State Director of the North Dakota Commission on Alcoholism, had been a friend of mine for a good many years. We had served together for years on the Board of Directors at Heartview Alcoholism Treatment Center.

Ken, our talkative family doctor, was my pillar of strength and personal friend. Sandy-haired and slightly balding, he always had his stethescope draped around his neck or in his pocket wherever he went.

It was the following spring when the three of us got re-acquainted. The honesty, sincerity, and effectiveness of their Christian lives helped me see how stifling and deadly was my narrow-minded emphasis on the charismatic experience *per se.* I now believe in a creative, active God who is involved in *all* of life—not just in the six or seven areas I had assigned to Him. Ever since boyhood, and especially in my career as an ad man, I had been challenged to create new ideas—new ways of doing things. I can hardly believe that I had allowed myself to accept such a stereotyped, narrow concept of God.

As I write this, I am convinced that no mere human can define the limits of God's power, beauty, or methods. I'm glad that He gets bigger each time I meet with Him. I'm thankful He doesn't let me get permanent handles on my understanding of Him. I'm thankful that He challenges me frequently to re-think my theological position. I'm excited about the way He works with each of us as an individual—not with people in lumps.

In addition to helping me get my spiritual life in perspective, Bernie and Ken gave me something else I needed and longed for: honest, down-to-earth Christian fellowship. How I thank God for that!

With several other men who had the same need and the same longing, we started meeting weekly to share our love for the Lord and our struggle to live the life He wants for us. We were not concerned with rules, doctrines, objectives, evangelism, or methods of worship. We came together for the strength and reinforcement we found in honest fellowship with others who loved God.

In addition to our church congregations, all of us needed a home, a place to belong, a small group of people who would surround us with their love and their commitment to help us grow—a gathering of fellow believers to share with, identify with, and grow with. Such a gathering is a *church* in the truest sense of the word.

But there is much confusion about the meaning of that word *church*. To many, it is an institution, a building, an exclusive social club, a weekly style show—something to do or something to go to. How shallow our definitions! The Church is far more than any of these. It is a diverse body of believers who claim Jesus Christ as their Savior and their Master. It is an invisible body of visible, human servants who spend themselves in healing, suffering, ministering, teaching, and witnessing.

For me, the Church is even more than that. It is a group of representatives and ambassadors for Christ, whose love for their King is greater than all doctrine, religion, denominationalism, politics, social class, and theology.

But even a church of this kind can be effective only when it begins with acknowledgement of its sins and earnest repentance. As an individual, I must repent personally. As the Church, we must repent collectively—for not sharing the full message given to us by Jesus Christ, for neglecting the needs of others, for selfishness, for our lack of concern with justice, for amassing church wealth beyond our needs, and for hundreds of other sinful acts and thoughts.

I believe such a humble, repentant church will survive and increase as its members deliberately surrender to the power and guidance of the Holy Spirit. And that type of firm commitment and surrender can come only in an honest, open, confronting, loving community. It is these communities that give life to the church—the life it so desperately needs.

In sizing up the problems of the groups I had worshipped with earlier, I came to one firm conclusion. All of them had arrived at their positions through their use and interpretation of the Bible. The way a man uses, interprets, and understands the Bible usually determines the way in which he lives out his Christian life.

The importance of the Bible and its centrality in the life of a Christian cannot be overemphasized. It is our life—our bread. Without it we have nothing. Each minute I spend studying the Bible, whether I feel like it or not—is rewarding, refreshing, and encouraging.

As I come to the Bible, however, I need to recognize that I have my own way of interpreting it. Whether I admit it or not, I really interpret the Bible every time I read it. I bring to the Bible a value system—my own experiences, ideas, and theology. I bring to the Bible my own built-in method of interpretation. If my method of interpretation is wrong, my applications will also be wrong.

There was a time when I searched the Bible only to find more proof for my own position. Consequently, I didn't allow the Bible to speak to me objectively. I was more concerned with deductively finding new "proof texts" to convert others to my way of thinking. I was seldom concerned with finding God's whole truth for me. I neglected many dimensions of the Christian faith because I wanted the Bible to comfort me where I was—not disturb me about where I wasn't.

Wanting to find justification from my own theology, I often wrote off certain passages as irrelevant, while giving other passages top priority. My Christianity was actually based on a few Scripture verses, not on the broader dimensions of the whole Bible. When I saw that, it was a painful revelation. But I had to see it if I was to grow in my faith.

Eventually I realized that there is no really *pure* interpretation of the Bible. Every translation of the Bible is an interpretation in itself. That's why it is my responsibility as a Christian to read many different translations, in order to get the full thrust and meaning of a specific passage. As a Christian, I am commanded to be studious. (The word *disciple* means "pupil.") There is no easy way out.

When we interpret the Bible, we must "test the spirits" to see whom we're listening to. If the fruit of our biblical interpretation is love, then we can rest assured that we have interpreted correctly. But if we wind up being more concerned with such side issues as demons, fasting, "correct" doctrine, and imposing our views on others, then we need to look upon that interpretation with a critical, cautious eye.

As some of these principles became clearer to me, I found myself praying more and more, "Lord, help me get off this doctrinal kick. Give me a *ministry* where I can show Your love to those who are unloved by others."

And I had a hunch that the answer to my prayer was just around the corner.

Chapter 9

*For I am not ashamed of this
Good News about Christ.
It is God's powerful method
of bringing all who believe
it to heaven ...
This Good News tells us that God makes
us ready for heaven—makes us
right in God's sight—when we put our
faith and trust in
Christ to save us. This is
accomplished from start
to finish by faith.*

Romans 1:16, 17a (TLB)

All These Hurting People

I kept thinking about the kid I had talked with in the pizza joint just before going to seminary. The question he had asked haunted me incessantly: "What are you doing about all these hurting people?"

The answer was always the same: "Nothing—*yet*. But I will."

Even while in seminary, I had been checking out all the Christian youth organizations I knew about. In the process of writing letters, talking with friends, and looking over different church groups, I finally came across Young Life. After carefully comparing it with the other organizations I knew of, this seemed to appeal to me more than any other.

Bill, a fellow-seminarian who was studying for the priesthood, and Jeff, a friend who was working on his master's in theology, introduced me to the regional staff people in Minneapolis. As I talked with these men, I was overwhelmed at their dedication to Christ and young people. As far as I could see, they were committed for life.

I was especially impressed with Phil McDonald, the Regional Director for the Midwest. He was a real man's man: slim, tall, and bearded, with big hands, big heart and a Texas accent. The amazing thing was his sincere interest in me—even though we'd just met. I soon learned that this concern for the personal needs of each person he meets is what endears him to the hearts of so many young people.

Phil explained Young Life to me more fully. As I listened to his animated explanations, and saw the enthusiasm in his expressive eyes, I knew I was sitting in the presence of a man who'd found out what God's love is all about. Phil and all the Young Life staff men seemed to have so much love, wisdom and dedication. The organization was just a way of channeling that love in the right direction.

I learned that Young Life is an international, interfaith organization which specializes in low-key evangelism for kids. Their whole strategy is based on an almost-casual, one-to-one contact with kids by Young Life workers. This kind of evangelism is much different from the traditional, Bible-waving hell-fire kind I'd heard of. It's based on loving the other person with no strings attached. There are no high pressure tactics. The "evangelist" almost seems to be loafing: roving around with the kids, making friends, helping them with their problems, looking for an opportunity to share Christ.

Then there are the clubs: informal rapping sessions which just naturally grow out of the friendships formed in the initial contacts. It is here where many of the kids are able to get their problems talked out, and come to know Christ personally.

I liked the camping program too. It's in the camps where the kids really get a chance to meet the Lord in a creative way, to grow in their faith and develop maturity and leadership.

I knew that no specific prayer group, church group, school, or youth organization could care for the needs of all young people. But as I listened to Phil McDonald, Young Life seemed to be the one that appealed to me as most creatively meeting the spiritual needs of the greatest number of teen-agers.

Now, back in North Dakota, I knew the time had come for action. I contacted Phil and told him I was ready. Under his supervision, I would begin a full-time Young Life ministry in Bismarck.

From the beginning, God sent people to help. The first one was Becky. A local college student and an attractive, red-headed, bubbly Christian, she did much of the necessary office work.

Young Life had been well established for many years in other parts of the country, but it had never been heard of in this state. Without much promised support (Young Life is financed by local contributions), we decided to forge ahead, trusting God to provide for our needs and guide us in our work.

Having come to this ministry through prayer and providential circumstances, it was a great feeling for me to know that I was doing what God wanted me to do, where He wanted me to do it. After fighting Him for so long, it was a great relief to have such peace.

Early in this ministry, I learned that our geographic location makes little difference. God will work with us wherever we are. Since my conversion, I had always wanted to get into some big-time ministry in the cities, to do the sort of work that famous men like Dave Wilkerson, Tom Skinner, and Bill Milliken have done. North Dakota seemed to me to be the spiritual desert of the world. In time, God helped me to understand that I was needed right where I was, to create (with Him) the spiritual environment that didn't exist in this area. Slowly my attitude was changed, and I began to see my mission in North Dakota as an opportunity and an exciting challenge that no city could offer.

After several meetings with the Bismarck High School administration, I was finally given permission to come to the school during students' free times. My approach to the school officials had brought up the usual questions regarding separation of church and state. It was finally decided that our contact work did not infringe on the separation, since our work on the school grounds was geared mostly to the building of friendships rather than the presentation of the Gospel message. After a thorough investigation of the Young Life program, the school officials were very supportive. They were sincerely concerned about the kids and their welfare, and were willing to do anything that might help alleviate some of the problems being encountered in high schools.

With those details out of the way, I was ready to launch the first phase of Young Life's work. That was to get acquainted with the kids and find out what their needs were. The first time I went to the high school for this purpose, I was so scared I wanted to turn around and run. I didn't know how the kids would interpret an adult's invasion of their world.

Sitting in the crowded cafeteria, decorated with pictures of famous rock stars, I felt my heart go out in compassion as I saw hundreds of lonely, hurting, unloved kids. This was a world of pain I had not been familiar with—pain so overwhelming that I had no idea how to begin to deal with the many needs that only Jesus could meet.

I began by gathering names of kids who seemed to need a friend. I soon found that the list was endless. Following the pattern that Jesus set in approaching each person individually, I asked God to guide me to one teen-ager at a time. I prayed that they would be open to me in my friendship. On a consistent, daily basis, my prayers were answered and, one by one, kids began to accept me. At first, they were skeptical about an older person coming to the high school, but as time went on, more and more of them began to trust me. I guess they believed in me because I was consistent and persistent in my desire to get to know them.

Within a few months, I had decided to focus on about forty needy kids. I did everything I could to gain their friendship and went wherever I could to be with them—at athletic events, in the school, in after-school hangouts, and in their homes.

As these relationships developed, we began a club—the second phase of Young Life's approach. It grew fast because kids were aware that that Club had something real to offer them.

No youth leader is ever content with the work he does, even if he spends twenty hours a day at it. The needs I kept discovering were so tremendous that my work was hardly scratching the surface. I continued to meet with kids prayerfully and consistently, hoping to recruit and train other people to do the things I was doing.

For several months, I prayed for an opportunity to meet seven of the boys whom I considered the biggest pushers and users of dope in the high school. One morning I got to the school, as usual, around ten-thirty. In the corridor, I ran into Gus, one of the "Big Seven." He was probably the hardest-looking guy I had ever met. After speaking to him, I noticed that he held a portfolio filled with paintings—some of his recent art-class creations. I asked to see them. Reluctantly, he began to show them to me and, as I expressed genuine interest, to explain their meaning.

I was so excited to be with Gus, so excited about God's answer to prayer, that I was pretty oblivious to what was going on around us. In a few minutes, two other guys came up to inspect the work, and soon afterwards four others joined them. As we stood there in the dark hallway peering at Gus's artwork, I suddenly realized that these were the seven I had been praying for—all gathered there in one spot!

When we had pretty well exhausted the subject of art, one of the fellows asked me belligerently why the hell I was there.

"I'm here because I love kids, and I want to show them I do," I answered a little shakily.

"We've heard that line before," was the reply.

"I know you have," I responded apologetically. "I'm sorry it doesn't mean anything to you. . . ."

Another guy suddenly said, "I heard you talk on TV the other night, about Young Life or something like that. What kind of a damn weirdo group is that?"

"It's not for weirdos—it's for guys like you and me. It's a club that shares ideas about life. Anything wrong with that?"

"What ideas about life?" he asked.

I began to tell them that God loved them, that He cared about their lives, that He wanted to give them happiness. That line, too, was one they had heard before—and they began to bombard me with a series of salty comments and difficult questions. Finally one of the boys said, "And you—who do you think you are? Why are you in this racket? What the hell is in it for you?"

"Nothing is in it for me—nothing at all," I said. "I just know from experience that there's more to life than getting stoned, laying chicks, and making money."

For some reason, that statement got their attention, and for twenty minutes I had an opportunity to share with these guys and to listen to what they had to say. I left there praising God for the seeds He had allowed me to plant. Many of these seeds took root. Out of these seven hard-core drug users, five are now Christians.

But every exciting, positive experience was matched with a negative, depressing one. Among the kids I have worked with, some continue to take dope; some have committed suicide; some continue to find their meaning in sex; some still get their kicks out of destroying property and rebelling against their parents and the system; some are now in prisons; some who accepted Christ have gotten mixed up with bad companions; some dump their faith when times get tough. In some cases, I've failed to spend time with kids who needed my time; in other cases, I've given up on kids because they rejected me and what I stand for. But those failures just make me try harder and stimulate me to think of newer, creative ways to reach more young people.

Some of the failures have been of my own making. Take John, for example.

John's attitude was hostile from the time I met him He had heard about Young Life and didn't dig the program.

As we were walking to the parking lot one cold afternoon, he challenged me with some of his ideas: "Jesus was an anarchist. I know He was. He never belonged to a political party. He never believed in the system. Jesus was an anarchist, and that's why I'm one. He's my leader."

Because I was too cold and too concerned about getting to my next appointment to give John the attentive hearing his statement deserved, I responded by telling him that I thought his interpretation of the Bible was wrong.

"I should have known what you'd say," he sneered. "You're just another one of those white, Anglo-Saxon, establishment-type preachers. You don't see the truth. You don't see that this whole —— system has to be overthrown. Maybe some day you'll see the light."

I failed with John because I argued with him instead of listening to what he had to say and then sharing with him the love of Jesus and the powerful message of the Gospel.

The last I heard, John was attending some Ivy League school and was "kickin' the hell out of those establishment bastards."

Another kid that I failed with is Joan. My first encounter with her was by telephone. She called late one night to ask if I was "the guy who works with kids." When I acknowledged that I was, she laid it on the line:

"Listen, man, I need help. I've heard that you're willing to help kids. I'm a real bitch. I want you to know that. Nobody reaches me. I've been the gamut, but I need an out."

With more confidence than I felt, I replied, "I've dealt with your kind before. No sweat. When do you wanna meet?"

"I'll meet you at the school lunchroom at two tomorrow. OK?"

"OK," I replied. "Tell me how I'll know you."

After she had described herself and told me what she'd be wearing, I hung up the phone and asked for God's involvement in our meeting.

Two o'clock the next afternoon found me in the lunchroom, looking over a sea of kids in the hope of spotting a redhead with wire rims, blue jeans, and a plaid shirt. It was a little bit like looking for a particular pebble on a beach full of them.

I heard someone behind me call my name. Turning, I found that Joan's self-description was accurate. Her self-image, however, was poor. In our conversation that afternoon she kept insisting that she was a bitch and that nothing could change her.

"Do you really think that about yourself, Joan?"

"Why the hell should I feel any different? My parents hate me. My brothers and sisters are ashamed of me. Listen, man, I'm sixteen years old. I'm a year behind in school. I can't hold down a job. I'm dating a married man. I've been to every counseling place in the area. They keep telling me I gotta change."

As I opened my mouth to reply, she hastily added, "And don't lay that —— God trip on me. I'm sick of religion and that Sunday school talk."

As tears began rolling down her cheeks, she continued, "I'm a nobody ... a failure. I don't give a damn about anything. I dare you—I dare you to tell me I'm worth something!"

I waited until the sobbing had quieted, and then asked, "What specifically prompted you to call me?"

"I need help. I need *help!* I can't stand myself anymore. I feel so ugly and dirty inside. I gotta change. I just gotta."

She hesitated and then went on. "I'm pregnant—at least I think I am. I need an abortion. Can you help me make arrangements?"

"Joan," I said, "I know someone you can talk to. A great girl who's had experiences like yours. Maybe she can help you more than I can."

Her reaction startled me. The weeping changed to rage. "You're no different," she stormed at me. "You're just like every other counselor I've ever had. Every one of you is the same." Abruptly she started walking away. I hurriedly followed her and begged her to explain what she meant.

"Every time I meet with you counselors—or

whatever you guys call yourselves," she replied sarcastically, "you end up sending me to someone else. Can't you understand that I'm sick and tired of being shoved around? I want someone to stick with me—someone who's willing to live through these things with me. All you guys ever do is foist me off on someone else. I can't take it any more! I'm fed up!" With that, she ran away.

I went to my office, trying to figure out some way to deal with kids like Joan, who had been through every other program available. For some reason, our place was where the buck stopped. We spent a lot of time locating homes, apartments, "crash pads," jobs, and counselors for kids who had no place to belong.

I knew what's involved in making a commitment to another person. It means giving everything you've got to see that person through. I decided to call Joan to let her know that I was willing to make this sort of commitment to her.

When she came to the phone, I apologized for suggesting that she talk to another person. There was no response.

"Joan, listen to me," I persisted. "I care about you. I care about your situation. I want to help. I will do everything to see you through this thing."

Tearfully, she agreed to see me again. I could sense, from the tone of her voice, that she felt acceptance and that she had been touched by my offer.

For several weeks, I met with Joan for at least one hour each week. At the last of those meetings, Joan told me she had made arrangements for her abortion. I tried to get her to see the other side, but she wouldn't listen to me. As we left the smoky high school hangout, I asked Joan for a couple more minutes.

"Joan," I said, "do you remember saying you needed someone to go through everything with you? Do you remember talking about someone being with you all the time?"

"You've helped me, Ron. You've really helped me, but you aren't there when I need you most. You can't be with me late at night or early in the morning. There's no way you can be at my side when I can't sleep."

"That's what I mean, Joan. I know that. But I do know Someone who loves you much more than I do. Someone who cares about every part of your life. Someone who'll be with you all the time."

She nodded as if she were following everything I said. "Joan," I said, "Jesus wants to give you His life."

Joan burst into tears—but they were not tears of repentance "I guess I was right from the beginning," she sobbed. "you *don't* understand me. You *are* just like the rest. I told you

you'd never reach me—and I was right. You can't take it. You haven't got the guts to stick it out with me. You want to force me off on someone else. Can't you see that I need someone *human* to be with me? That Jesus-in-the-sky crap is for religious pimps. Not for me!"

As she tried to run away, I grabbed her arm. "Joan," I said, "don't you understand? I'd never be here with you if I didn't know that Jesus loves you. He got me into this work so that I could be available to you. Do you buy that?"

Obviously she didn't. Her mind was closed to the idea, and nothing would open it.

"See you sometime, Ron," she said as she pulled away from me.

"When?" I asked.

"Sometime . . . sometime," she said.

I thought about our encounter as I drove home. Why had she rejected Jesus? What had gone wrong? I was sure that the timing had been right.

For several weeks afterward, my mind turned to Joan and her situation every time it wasn't occupied with an immediate problem. I tried to call her on the phone and to see her at the high school, but she avoided me. She had written me off—perhaps forever.

John and Joan are just two of hundreds of personal failures on my list—failures because of my own impatience and stupidity. I've had kids threaten me, challenge me, try me, question me, shove me, tempt me. But deep inside they know that, if what I proclaim is the truth, I'll come back for more. And I do.

It's not the mechanics of establishing a Christian ministry that make it hard. It's the intangible, spiritual problems that gnaw at the foundation of my personal spiritual life.

At first, some of these intangibles didn't worry me too much. As time went on, however, I became more and more concerned about the impact they were having on my life.

The loss of close friends ... the rejections and negative comments by those who seemed to be supporters ... the phony back-patters ... the lack of support ... adult Christians and kids dumping their faith ... ministers quitting their jobs ... sick theology ... criticism and jealousy from other Christians ... harassing phone calls ... negative comments from church leaders ... the struggle to keep my own integrity ... the trauma of seeing kids killing themselves everyday with drugs, alcohol, and other destructive weapons provided by our society.

Trials like these a Christian worker can endure only through prayer and the grace of God.

There are times when I can hardly bear to listen to some of the stories the kids want to share with me.

Karen telling me her dad tried to "make her."

Rich telling me he's "not ready yet to sur-render because of all the fun he has with dope."

Mary telling me she's not capable of surren-dering her "beauty and cheerleading to God."

Peter telling me that "politics is where it's at."

Young people telling me that they are too ugly for anyone to love.

John telling me that "revolution is the key to life."

Pam telling me that "loving my brother is lov-ing God."

Sam telling me that "Christianity is a white man's religion."

Susie telling me that guys "give her every-thing she needs."

Paula telling me that the church is the only "source of life"—the ultimate source of all truth.

Juicers telling me that the sauce is better than any God.

Fred asking why he has V.D. if God really loves him.

College kids who had accepted Christ writing to say they've "found something better than Jesus."

Bill asking how God reveals himself in a neighborhood permeated with poverty and all its ills.

Gloria asking how God could possibly love a cripple "when no one else does."

Laurie telling me she has no place to live.

Scott looking for a way to make friends in a strange town.

Marty proclaiming all the benefits of witchcraft.

Lisa weeping about her alcoholic father.

Carol shouting "You gotta be hip—get off the Jesus thing."

Steve saying, "The Christian life was OK while it lasted. That's not for me any more."

Tom saying, "I'm a jock. What more do I need?"

Jim crying because he doesn't "have a friend—not one real friend."

Rich saying "The only guys who really care about me are dopers."

Kids beaten by enraged or drunken parents.

Judy crying about her father's extramarital affair.

Don worried about his minister's illicit relationship with a married woman.

Ken's feelings of being neglected by his father, who is trying "to make it big in the business world."

Candy crying because her mother is always away from home, "earning money for a new dishwasher" while she is left alone.

Susan embarrassed about her mother's "radical involvement in Women's Lib."

Ted worried about how he will ever be accepted, since the word is out that he's a homosexual.

Ten-year-olds running away from home. Fourteen-year-olds having affairs with perverted married men. Fifteen-year-olds having babies.

Kids screaming for their parents' attention through drug use and sex abuse.

Lower-class kids longing to be upper-class kids. Upper-class kids trying to look like lower-class kids.

Kids going to after-school religion classes drunk, loaded, and blitzed.

Georgia crying about her parents' divorce.

David abandoned by his parents.

Susie telling me, "It's hard to pray in my room when cockroaches keep distracting me."

Jake trying to convince me that he "will never kick dope."

Rural kids too shy to say anything more than their names.

Jim, after overdosing intentionally three times, telling me that he's all right; "everyone else is screwed up."

Retarded kids crying because everyone laughs at them.

Handicapped kids feeling "left out."

Curt asking how he can break into the "neat crowd," since he isn't funny, studly, or musically talented.

Grant yelling about the hyprocrisy of the church.

Six kids riding in an Eldorado talking about how they will implement a revolution in a system that is unjust.

JoAnn feeling that Jesus will never forgive her for "the terrible thing she did Friday night."

Andy waiting for a specific sign from God (a new car) before he will give his life to Him.

Jeff afraid of what he might have to give up if he becomes a Christian.

John questioning how God can allow a criminal to be confined to fifteen years in prison.

I have had many a dark night in this ministry. At one time, I recall having less than a dime in my pocket, no gas in my car, many overdue bills, not one friend I could talk to, and no promise of support for our program. Few kids were coming to our activities, and many parents were upset over what they were hearing about Young Life. The Bible wouldn't speak to me, and God seemed far away.

I don't understand why Christians have these periods. All I know is that they drove me to my knees. Even though prayer brought me no comfort, God must have heard me. At least He kept the ministry going.

At the end of many a trying day, I have turned to the Bible and found comfort in Saint Paul's words to the Christians in Corinth:

132

We are in difficulties on all sides, but never cornered; we see no answer to our problems, but never despair; we have been persecuted, but never killed; always, wherever we may be, we carry with us in our body the death of Jesus, so that the life of Jesus, too, may always be seen in our body. (2 Corinthians 4:8-10)

My "fanaticism" and my involvement in Young Life have cost me many friends. A loss of one friend in particular—a person I had been exceptionally close to—has really grieved me.

One day not so long ago, I asked my secretary to give me a list of all the kids we had closely worked with during the year. We were planning to do something special for this group's graduation. When Sarah brought the list in, I counted the names on it. There were exactly 100. Each of these hundred kids was a close friend of mine.

I opened the Bible to look for some appropriate passages to share with this group. Reading through the Gospel of Matthew, I encountered verse 29 in chapter 19: "And everyone who has left houses, brothers, sisters, father, mother, children or land for the sake of my name will be repaid *a hundred times over*, and also inherit eternal life." I had lost a friend; but in just one year I had literally acquired a hundred new ones because of Christ. After reflecting on that verse, I knew what I would be sharing with these kids.

The rewards of working in a youth ministry

cannot be measured or described. Perhaps the greatest earthly rewards come from kids who begin to give back to us—kids who stick with the Christian faith, develop in their own way, and begin to share their discoveries with us—kids like Jim, Becky, and Sarah, who have been through the non-Christian gamut, have been converted, and are now ministering to me and to other teen-agers. I praise God for them. They care because someone cared for them—cared enough to reach out to them, to meet them at a game, bring them to a club, take them to a camp, and listen to their problems. They give because someone gave to them.

To Becky, Jim, Sarah, and others like them, John's words are very much alive:

We know how much God loves us because we have felt his love and because we believe him when he tells us that he loves us dearly. God is love, and anyone who lives in love is living with God and God is living in him. And as we live with Christ, our love grows more perfect and complete; so we will not be ashamed and embarrassed at the day of judgment, but can face him with confidence and joy, because he loves us and we love him too. (1 John 4:16, 17, TLB).

Chapter 10

My children,
our love is not to be
just words
or mere talk,
but something real and active.

1 John 3:18

How Do You Express Love?

Loneliness has been a recurring problem for me since the beginning of my Christian life. If one is seriously committed to the Lord and the work of His kingdom, he will inevitably experience this. Saints of old have written about it. Biblical characters have cried and prayed about it. Any honest Christian admits that it is his experience also.

The only solution that I found is to cry honestly to God from the bottom of my heart, letting Him know that I need His nearness.

During the times when my loneliness seemed almost too much to bear, three thoughts have comforted me. The first is that Jesus understands my suffering, since He experienced the ultimate in loneliness as He hung on the cross. Deserted by most of His disciples, He also felt forsaken by the Father. I have sometimes echoed His cry of despair, *"My God, my God, why have you deserted me?" (Matthew 27:46).*

It is also comforting to realize that many other Christians have experienced loneliness just as great as mine. As Saint Paul said, *"Many others have faced exactly the same problems before you. And no temptation is irresistible. You can trust God to keep the temptation from becoming so strong that you can't stand up against it, for he has promised this and will do what he says." (1 Corinthians 10:13, TLB).*

Third, I find comfort in knowing that Jesus is capable of doing something powerfully constructive with my burden of loneliness when I lay it before Him—*"for when the way is rough, your patience has a chance to grow" (James 1:3, TLB).*

Closely related to the problem of loneliness has been the problem of unfulfilled sexual desires. My struggle with these two temptations has taught me the power that comes from surrendering completely to God. I learned—at long last—that I could trust Him for *all* my needs, including my need for a wife.

God knows our make-up and our desires—and in His own way and His own good time, He provides for those desires which are in accordance with His plan for our lives. I had spent many hours in prayer trying to coerce God into giving me this or that girl for a wife. I was tired of waiting for His choice, and on a few occasions

I gave up the idea that He would provide a wife for me at all. At such times, I would start dating a girl who seemed to me a likely candidate. Those relationships never worked out, and I finally realized that my marriage would be a failure if I married a girl who was not God's choice for me.

Reluctantly, I surrendered that part of my life to God. It was the corner that was most difficult to give up. I liked being master of my love life.

It was just before I reached this point of surrender that Mary Beth came back into my life. I had first met her while she was in college and had been drawn to her even then by her beautiful black hair and brown eyes. She seemed so sweet, pure, and innocent that I immediately classified her as the "little sister type." Just before her junior year, the year she spent in France, we developed a wholesome relationship.

It was shortly after her return home that I ran into her again. The more I saw of her, the more I was impressed by her kindness, her uniqueness, and her love for the Lord. I could sense that she was drawn to me, as I was to her.

It was about then that I surrendered my love life to God—and above everything else, I wanted our relationship to be pleasing to Him. Without the other's knowledge, Mary Beth and I were each laying fleeces before the Lord, asking Him to make it very obvious if He was the one who was bringing us together. After that, I don't believe we ever spent time together without His approval. Each time we met, it was through His arrangement.

We soon found that we were compatible intellectually, emotionally, socially, and—best of all—spiritually. Mary Beth not only spoke French and Russian; she also spoke in tongues.

Through a long series of miraculous encounters, I became convinced Mary Beth was God's choice for my wife. When I asked her to marry me, she accepted without hesitation.

Because I had waited (although not without fussing and fighting), God gave me the very beautiful, creative Christian wife He knew I needed. Only He could deliver precisely the life companion that my personality called for.

It is impossible to describe the beauty and the blessing of having a wife like Mary Beth to share in the ministry to which God has called us. Together we work with kids and with others who need us. Mary Beth has her own special ministry, dealing mostly with married women.

Like most couples, Mary Beth and I have occasional communication gaps in our relationship. These are usually my fault and stem from the fact that I am a "workaholic" and have not yet learned to be sensitive to my wife's moods and needs.

If the status of sainthood were given to wives who put up patiently with insensitive husbands, my wife's canonization papers would be here any day.

At the end of one hectic week, Mary Beth and I managed to find a few minutes for prayer together. "Would you like to pray first?" I asked.

"Yes," she replied, "but can I first talk to you about something that's bothering me?"

At this danger signal, my heart sank—but I tried to sound cheerful and confident as I said, "Sure."

"Ron," she began hesitantly, "you keep talking about love and all the other stuff that goes with it. You keep talking about expressing love and fulfilling needs. May I ask a selfish question?"

Bracing myself for the punch line, I nodded.

"Ron, how do you express your love for me?"

Her question hit me like a ton of bricks. I knew that Mary Beth had every right to feel neglected, and that no explanation would be adequate. When a man loves a woman, it should be obvious that he does. He shouldn't have to explain it with words.

Jesus was using Mary Beth to show me something about myself that He had often tried to get me to see: that I am much better at talking the talk than at walking the walk. Mary Beth wanted me to *spend some time with her*, not just tell her in passing that I love her. She wanted me to sit with her, to listen to her, to share with her, to do things with her. She wanted to be involved in every part of my life—to hear about my plans, programs, ideas, fantasies, and dreams. As was my lifelong habit, I had conveniently revealed to her only what I wanted to reveal.

Basically, Mary Beth was asking of me what Christ asks of all his followers. To be sure, He wants us to express our love for Him by tangible acts of kindness to His brothers (see Matthew 25:31-46); but He also wants us to spend time with Him and with His word (see Luke 10:38-42). He wants to be involved in our activities—all of them. He wants us to share our dreams with Him.

Mary Beth and I talked and prayed together for about three hours. During that time, I not only learned a lot about myself and my marriage, I also received a new perspective on my relationship with Christ.

I keep learning many other things from Mary Beth and from our marriage. We praise God daily that we have each other. We're more dedicated to each other than ever before. Not the least important thing I have learned, however, is that no human companionship—not even marriage to a mate of God's own choosing—can end the loneliness that is part of our existence on earth. Only God can *completely* fill the vacuum that He put in each person's soul.

And one more thing: I think I've finally learned a little more about the kind of love that kids need too—thanks to God and Mary Beth.

Chapter 11

*'Anyone who wants to become
great among you must be your servant,
and anyone who wants to be first among
you must be slave to all.
For the Son of Man himself did not come to
be served but to serve, and
to give His life as a ransom for many.*

Mark 10:43-45

Kids Need Time

In working with kids, I used to think I had all the answers for all their problems. Now I know better. It gets more difficult each year to develop programs that will appeal to all kids. The culture of youth is too complex for easy answers. Generalizations about teen-agers no longer make sense. I am both encouraged and bewildered by the great diversity in their attitudes and life styles. That diversity has challenged me to look at each young person as a unique individual, with specific needs and problems, who can be reached only by a very creative approach to the Gospel.

One generalization I can make is that all teen-agers need genuine relationships. Buildings, committees, school activities, and programs have an appeal for some kids. But mostly, kids want friends. There is no substitute for real relationships. Because it is difficult to give of ourselves and easy to give of our resources, we adults have sought to solve youth problems the easy way—by giving money instead of time.

For a while, I thought kids could be brought to Christ—the answer for all their needs—by a tract, a booklet, or a one-time proclamation of the Gospel. It took me a long time to learn that ministry is much more than passing out tracts; it's a relationship that's centered on lifelong commitment to the other person, regardless of response. To me, ministry means helping a kid understand all the factors in his life, encouraging him to sort them out and keep the perspective of Christ. I've learned that distribution of literature is only one small part of a ministry with kids.

Generally, I try to give kids what I think they need most—time, attention, example, and love.

Love is a word that means many things to many people. To me, it means giving unselfishly for the benefit of another person without expecting anything in return, ever. As a Christian, I have no right to expect anything in return for my love. If I am concerned about response, I deserve to be disappointed.

Most of all, kids need a real relationship with Christ. Every person I know needs that relationship, and it is surprising how many kids, underneath all the fear and hostility, really want a relationship with Christ. They want and need a Savior, Redeemer, Friend, and Lover. Someone who can be with them all the time. Only Jesus Christ—through His Holy Spirit—can fulfill that need.

I can't always keep kids from bad pitfalls, although I try to warn them. The mistakes kids make are often very costly, and every time I think of Bernie, I'm reminded of the importance of trying to steer kids straight.

Bernie was the friend I mentioned earlier— the State Director of the North Dakota Commission on Alcoholism—who had helped me so understandingly through my "superspiritual days."

Just a few days before his death, Bernie called me to his office to share with me two messages of vital importance to young people. This dedicated Christian, himself an arrested alcoholic, had devoted almost thirty years of his life to working with alcoholics. Now he knew that his life was almost over.

"Ron," he said, "I have made many mistakes in my life. Many of them you know about. But before I die, I want to share with you the two greatest mistakes I have made.

"When I was younger," he went on, "I believed that I could do anything that I wanted to—sow my wild oats, so to speak—without having to pay the consequences later. Even though I know I am forgiven for all I have done, I still carry scars for my past behavior—scars that will be with me until my death. Please encourage kids to live clean lives from their youth up—not to make the mistake of thinking they can get away with *anything* without paying the consequences."

I nodded silently, knowing from experience the truth of what he was saying. After resting a few moments to regain his strength, Bernie went on. "The other mistake is probably worse than the first, and it's a hard one for me to admit. As you know, I've traveled all over the world and have had countless opportunities to share the good news of Christ with people from many different backgrounds. For one reason or another, I have failed to do that until just recently. Hundreds of people—perhaps thousands—could have known the saving power of Christ if I had been courageous enough to witness to them.

"If I could do anything to persuade kids to live clean lives and to share their love for the Lord, I would do it. You are in a position to influence kids. Will you please tell them about my failures? Maybe they can learn from them."

Tears were in my eyes. As I thanked Bernie and left his office, I knew I had received a message from one of God's angels. Bernie died several days later. I am honoring his request to make his mistakes known, so that others may learn from them.

I understood what he was talking about. His

mistakes were my mistakes. I had made them time and again. Even though I had been sorry and been forgiven, the scars remain. The memories are gone, but the scars are there.

I made up my mind that I would pay any cost to give kids the kind of love they need. Few parents give their children time. By the same token, few parents give their children real love and guidance. And rare indeed are parents who introduce their children to Jesus and give them an understanding of the Christian faith and an example of Christian living.

Barb is one of the kids who first made me aware of these needs so many young people have. When she called and said she wanted to talk to me, I told her I'd meet her for a Coke. At the cafe we agreed upon, I found her sitting at a table, alone.

For a while, we just sat there playing with soda straws, each of us waiting for the other to say something. Finally, Barb blurted out, "I know my parents don't love me. I'm getting sick of their phony game."

As usual, I jumped to a conclusion before I really understood the problem this sixteen-year-old girl was trying to share with me.

"I'm sure they love you, Barb," I replied. "They probably don't express it the way you'd like. Just because they don't give you everything you want, or let you do everything you want to—that doesn't mean they don't love you."

"That's exactly the problem," she said. "They do give me everything I want. They don't care about me, so they let me do anything I want to. They never even ask me where I go or what I do."

"Barb," I said, "what have your parents done recently to make you think they don't love you?"

"Nothing—nothing at all. They *never* do anything, and that's the problem. Last weekend I told them I'd be away for three days. I didn't tell them where I was going or when I'd get back because they didn't ask me. I got home Monday morning at two o'clock. At breakfast that morning, they acted like I had never been away. They didn't even ask me where I had gone."

Tears welled up in her eyes as she continued, "I'm sick of them not caring. I've done everything wrong that I can, just to get their attention. I'm sick of myself and all the crazy things I do with boys. I want my parents to stop me. I want them to care enough to tell me to shape up. Can you understand that? They don't care enough even to question me. Does that make sense to you?"

It made sense to me. Barb was right. Her parents obviously *didn't* care. They were among the apalling number of parents who have copped out on the responsibilities of parenthood and who simply want to get rid of their kids, to get them out of the house at all costs.

As I saw more of Barb over the next few weeks, I suggested that she might find help in a small Bible study group, where kids meet for sharing as well as Bible study. (Young Life creates such groups as one important phase of its work with teen-agers.) Barb did find help in such a group—but it was a poor substitute for the love she should have received from her parents.

Fortunately, Barb's case is a somewhat extreme example of parental indifference. But there are many teen-agers who know that their parents are feeding them a line when they talk about love. The words are there, but not the loving concern that kids need.

Barb came to Christ because she needed love. Linda needed to quit having sex with her boyfriend. Joyce needed security. Becky needed something she wasn't finding in her church. Dennis needed someone to confide in. Linda wanted to experience something real. Steve needed to get away from a rigid, legalistic religion. Jackie was pregnant and needed guidance. Byron needed to quit shoplifting. Gene needed to quit smoking grass. Tim was all wrapped up in himself. Dan wanted to be secure about eternal life. Claudia needed stability. Ginny needed someone to assure her that she was worth something. Tom needed direction and a purpose in his life.

These and many other kids who came to Christ through our club meetings are now in full and part-time Christian ministries. But before any of them could make the "jump to Christ," they needed someone human to point the way—someone to hear them out. The Gospel incarnate.

It's been delightful to see the miraculous changes in so many kids. Take Marie, for instance. During her sophomore and junior years in high school, she was a sharp, straight-A student who had a lot of friends and was interested in remedying the ills of society. Marie believed in a God, but she didn't know what kind. Her language was terrible. She boasted that she was a humanistic activist. Her parents had taken her to church as a child, and then *sent* her to church until her junior high years. About that time, she had decided that God wasn't paying much attention to her problems—or anybody else's for that matter.

"But then," she reasoned, "why do we need God to work out our problems when we can solve them for ourselves?"

But in her senior year, some disturbing things

began to happen. She began to see some of the shortcomings of humanistic philosophy. Even though she understood the needs of mankind—especially the need for love—she realized that man's limited love is not enough. There had to be something more.

"Why am I here?" She kept asking herself. "I want to count for something, and be a part of something important. But what can one person do?"

More than once, she found herself praying, "God, help me, wherever You are." But no help seemed to come.

Then one cool, fall day, while she was sitting through a boring biology lecture, a friend gave her a slip of paper. She unfolded it and read the following message:

"If you don't come to Y.L. tonight, I hope your legs grow together."

Marie had heard rumors about Young Life and was more than a little curious. That evening, she and her sister showed up at the club. They came a little late, found a place on the floor toward the back of the room and warily joined in the singing. As she glanced around, though, she noticed that many of the faces were familiar, which helped her to relax.

After the singing, she listened attentively as I gave a brief message. When it was all over, she left as inconspicuously as possible. She wanted to get alone and think about what she'd heard.

The next evening, she came to another of our meetings where she heard more about this new life in Christ. After the meeting, her girlfriend gave her a ride home. When they pulled up in front of Marie's home in the old beat-up car, her friend began to talk about a beautiful experience she'd had.

"Just a few months ago," she said, "I found this new life these people are talking about. Believe me, it's exciting! I've never been happier. Marie," she went on, "you've been running your own life for quite a while. You know it's a mess. You know you're not happy. Why not give Jesus a chance to do something for you?"

"Well, uh—I don't know...." Marie began.

"Please think about it," her friend said, as she handed Marie a salvation booklet. "You're missing something great."

Marie went to her cluttered room and began to devour the words written in the booklet. Afterwards, she quietly and humbly fell to her knees. Her time had come.

"Lord Jesus," she prayed, "I don't know much about You. All I know is that I need You. I want You to come into me. Please show me the good life I've heard about."

That evening marked the beginning of a new life for Marie. From then on, she attended every club meeting we held. As she grew in faith, she began to see that God's plan for helping society did not consist in men's pulling themselves up by their own bootstraps. God seemed to be saying to her, "This is the answer—this is how to help others: let Me flow through you."

As graduation approached, Marie felt that God wanted to use her in some way, although she didn't know how. One day she stopped into my office to visit. We spent an hour talking, dreaming and praying.

"It'll all work out for you," I assured her as I handed her some literature I had sent for, for her. "Please glance over this and give it some thought."

The literature was an invitation from Teen Mission (Merritte Island, Florida) for young people to join in a summer church project in Venezuela.

Her heart seemed to leap when she read the literature later on. She could hardly think of anything more exciting than the possibility of helping others in a foreign country.

"I want to go. I can't wait to go," she repeated to herself again and again. Finally, she came and shared her thoughts with me.

"My father will be the only obstacle," she said. "He'll never let me go."

"You'd better discuss it with him," I suggested. "You'll need his approval before you can give this any serious consideration."

A few days later, Marie came to our apartment crying. "I'm going to run away," she sobbed to Mary Beth and me. "I hate my father. He is so unreasonable! He doesn't listen to me. He wants me to get a job to make money this summer. He doesn't understand."

It was a tough situation. As best we could, Mary Beth and I counseled with her about the importance of submitting to her father; then we prayed with her. After several hours, Marie went home with a different attitude.

"I'll live out what I believe," she said with tears running down her cheeks. "I'll love him like he's never been loved before. If he doesn't want me to go, I won't go."

At home that night, Marie asked God to help her. "If You want me to go, please tell me, Lord. If it's Your desire for me to go on this mission, please open the doors for me."

The next three weeks were tense. Marie did everything she could to serve her father. Her surrender to God's will gave her the freedom to love him regardless of what he decided.

Three days before the deadline, Marie again prayed. "Lord," she said, "I will not disobey my father. I will follow his advice. Tomorrow I'm going to ask him for the last time. Whatever he says about my going on this trip, I will accept as

Your will." That prayer was a difficult one for Marie to put into words.

The next day, sitting in her father's den, Marie approached the subject as adroitly as possible. "Dad," she said, "I've received the latest information on the trip to Venezuela. This is the medical and insurance information." She handed it to him, sat back in her chair and patiently waited for some kind of response from her gray-haired father.

After a few moments' silence, he looked at her with a sigh of disgust and said, "You can go to that God-forsaken land—but I hope you have a miserable summer!"

A great miracle had happened! Marie bubbled over with excitement. Tears rolled down her cheeks as she tried hard to refrain from embracing her dad.

Marie went and had a perfectly beautiful summer in Venezuela. Since her return, she has given numerous talks around the state of North Dakota about making your life count for God.

Marie has been a significant part of Young Life's growth in North Dakota. She has been very active in leadership. Through her efforts, several new clubs and Bible studies have been started. Her life's ambition is to serve God as a missionary nurse. That great aspiration began with a question: "God, why am I here?"

And then there was Jason. When I first met him, he was a junior at one of the parochial schools in Bismarck. I had seen him around at school activities. Many of the kids told me that he was a "hard guy."

"He's impossible to reach," they said. Maybe that's why I looked forward to getting to know him. I enjoyed seeing what God could do with an impossibility.

The first few times I tried to talk with him, he bluntly told me to "cram it." In that crass reaction, I saw more than a "hard guy." I saw a lonely, hurting, lost, bewildered kid.

Jason came from an underprivileged family. They had been through bankruptcy several times. They had experienced many setbacks because of serious illnesses, heart attacks, mental disorders, and burdensome diseases. Off and on, they had been the recipients of welfare payments. When I learned about all this, I wasn't surprised at Jason's swearing, heavy drinking, and rejection of authority.

After we had prayed for months, Jason was finally dragged to one of our fall clubs by a close friend who was concerned about him. Jason told us later that he was impressed by the warmth of our club meeting, but he wasn't ready to give us his sex life, shoplifting and other exciting escapades.

He and five of his friends had contrived a lucrative "fund-raising program." By stealing and selling all kinds of merchandise, they made enough money for their own personal needs and a few luxuries besides. (The luxuries consisted of drinking, carousing and "raising hell," as they called it.)

He was inwardly attracted to the genuine concern our kids showed for one another. Completely confused by such young people, he tried to impress them by talking about how much he could rip off, how much he could drink, and how many different chicks he could lay. Nobody condemned him. We all knew how much he needed help.

Over the Christmas vacation, Jason became very depressed. No one knew what was bugging him, although we found out later.

Late in the afternoon, on a cold, windy day during that Christmas season, Jason and a girlfriend entered an old white clinic building. Silently, they both rode the squeaky elevator to the top floor. Arriving in a dimly-lighted doctor's office, they both sat uneasily waiting for "Miss Jones's" name to be called. A friend had helped them make arrangements for this crucial appointment.

After "Miss Jones" was called into the doctor's inner office, Jason delivered a bitter ultimatum to God. "OK," he said as he flipped nervously through a dog-eared magazine, "if You love me like they say You do, then let's see You get me out of *this* mess!"

He knew there wasn't one chance in a hundred that she wouldn't be pregnant. They'd been together too many times. And all that morning sickness: he knew what *that* meant.

Twenty minutes later, the sixteen-year-old blond returned. "Let's go," she said with a sparkle in her eye.

Jason, hurriedly following her, said, "What's the report? What did he say?"

"It's OK," she replied. "You're clear."

He couldn't believe it. He was stunned. And afraid. Even *he* knew that you can't "use" God to cover up sin—that you can't fool around with girls and expect God to get you out of the mess. He decided he'd prayed a horrible prayer. He was so confused he didn't know whether to laugh or cry.

Sitting on his bottom bunk in his disorderly bedroom a few hours later, he kept asking himself, "God really loves *me*? Could this really be? God loves *me*?"

Completely overwhelmed, he dropped to his knees and cried out his sins to God. It was a tender moment that only he and God shared.

Following that encounter with Christ, Jason began attending Young Life on a regular basis. He really needed the friendship of people who cared about him just as he was—rough and un-polished—without imposing changes.

Without anyone saying a word to him, he gave up his "sexcapades" and his stealing. Gradually, without any real concerted effort, his language began to get cleaned up too.

Jason's new life has touched many others. In his own soft, quiet way, he reaches out to others who are still living in the sinful pleasures he left behind.

The transformation in Jason's life is indeed miraculous. He has received a much-needed scholarship for college. He has a Christian girlfriend. His relationship with his parents has improved. He is proud of his home and his family. He "looks out" for his brothers and sisters. They depend on him for advice and material things. Jason has seen many of his friends become Christians. These, and many other "ordinary miracles" prove that God is still in the business of changing lives.

This "hard guy turned soft" has been involved in Young Life's workcrew, Bible study leadership, clubs, and speaking engagements. He is planning to go on staff somewhere with Young Life as soon as an opening develops.

I recall one of the first times Jason attended Young Life. I was trying to challenge the kids with a strong statement about the Bible. "When you read this Book," I said, "if you don't get something out of it—if you don't find answers to life's questions—if it doesn't change your life—I'll eat it page by page at Scotty's Drive-In parking lot."

Jason, like hundreds of others, accepted that challenge. I haven't had to eat the Bible.

Chapter 12

We have been a pleasure-loving people,
dishonoring God's day picnicking,
and bathing—
now the seashores are barren;
no picnics, no bathing.
We have preferred motor travel to
churchgoing—now there is a shortage
of motor fuel....
The money we would not give to the Lord's
work—now is taken from
us in taxes and higher prices.
The food for which we forgot to say thanks—
now is unobtainable....
Nights we would not spend in "watching unto
prayer"—
now are spent in anxious air-raid
precautions.
—Unknown

The Day I Blew My Cool

When I accepted Christ, many people told me that the Christian life is an adventurous journey—and I have found it to be so. It's exciting to be a part of God's kingdom—to have a feeling of belonging to something far greater than I can comprehend.

But few people told me that the Christian life is also a life of struggling and suffering. The Bible makes this plain:

We must never get tired of doing good because if we don't give up the struggle we shall get our harvest at the proper time.

Galatians 6:9

My brothers, you will always have your trials but, when they come, try to treat them as a happy privilege; you understand that your faith is only put to the test to make you patient, but patience too is to have its practical results so

that you will become fully-developed, complete,
with nothing missing.
   James 1:2-4

So I do not attempt to hide the fact that the
Christian life has been hard for me. It's a battle,
a struggle, a constant challenge. But a worthy
one. I would not exchange the best of my non-
Christian days for the worst of my Christian
days.

One of the biggest challenges of this ministry
has been to get adults interested in supporting
it. Ken—the family doctor and friend whom I
mentioned earlier—became the man through
whom God began to reach other adults and give
them the vision of a youth ministry. But it
wasn't easy. Most adults just couldn't understand why we were so concerned about their
kids' problems. In fact, some adults refused to
believe that such problems existed.

Through Ken and a handful of other committed men, we began to develop a genuine concern
about kids and their needs. These people formed
a committee that meets frequently to formulate
a broader plan for reaching young people.

As time went on, more and more adults began
to see what we were doing, and to contribute
their time, talents, and financial aid. These people not only raised the funds to carry on the
work of Young Life and did all the public rela-

tions works, but also worked on building relationships with kids who needed them. They say they are getting more from this work than they are giving to it. Didn't Jesus say, *"Give, and there will be gifts for you"* *(Luke 6:38)*? It costs them something—their time, adult friendships, and vulnerability—but the returns are immeasurable. Even yet, though, there are many adults who don't understand—a fact which I realized afresh only recently.

Occasionally, I am required to do some contact work with businessmen in order to raise funds for our youth work. One Monday morning, I had an appointment for this purpose with the president of a large company, whom I will call Fred. Fred is a man who "seeks first the kingdom of God" and still is a successful businessman.

In his comfortable office, I tried to tell him about the kids we work with, and about some of their problems.

"Ron," he broke in, "you aren't trying to convince me that kids really have these kinds of problems, are you?"

"Fred, many kids not only have serious spiritual problems, but they have serious physical problems too: no food to eat, no decent place to live," I said as convincingly as I could. "Some of them have no parents to care about them. Others have personality problems. The list is endless."

As one prestigious, wealthy man, Fred simply couldn't understand what I was saying. He thought I was feeding him a line—putting him no.

In my usual crass way, I proceeded to tell him that it is difficult for anyone who lives in a beautiful home, walks on thick carpets, wears fine clothing, and eats good food—"Fred, it's impossible for those living on this high standard to understand what happens in the other world.

"Fred, I'd be lying to you if I didn't tell you about these things. I'd be dishonest if I told you only the good things about kids. We are in trouble. We need to reach kids *now*. We are at a crisis point. There is a great urgency to do something before it is too late."

Still unconvinced, Fred handed me a check—a generous one.

"Before I really believe all that you're saying," he told me, "I need to experience it for myself. I need to see these things with my own eyes."

I love this man, and I want him to see the other dimension in life. I offered to take him with me any time he was available. He said he'd call, but he never has. Perhaps he's been too busy—or perhaps he's afraid to face the facts. (I'll be calling him.)

The things I was relating to Fred aren't secrets; they are common knowledge among Christian workers and social workers. We see hundreds of hungry, fatherless, impoverished kids. According to the Gospels, these are the people Jesus spent most of His time with. These are the people He calls us to minister to.

Too often we have seen innocent kids get ripped off by unscrupulous promoters of high-priced rock concerts, by drug pushers, and by car dealers. We have seen naive kids wrongly influenced by movies, books, and other forms of pornography.

I am aware of the reports that condone the use of drugs, and the justification they give to kids for the use of each drug. I don't care what those reports say. All drug abuse has long-range, devastating effects, and the legalization of those drugs is no solution to the problem. We have seen hundreds of lives destroyed by alcoholism and other forms of drug dependence. We have spent much time with kids whose lives have been ruined by prison sentences which were the direct or indirect result of drug use.

We see the increasing interest in Eastern religions and occult practices among young people. Yoga, Krishnaism and other forms of Hinduism, Buddhism, Bahaism, Transcendental Meditation, devil worship, Ouija boards, ESP, and astrology: several million people in America have dabbled in one or more of these dangerous practices. Their impact on our culture—and on young people especially is startling.

Only those who are both blind and naive deny that there is a spirit of revolution and destruction abroad in the land. We are sitting on top of a seething volcano that threatens to erupt at any time and spill out all manner of violence and tragedy.

The unbelievable increases in divorce, alcoholism, drug addiction, suicide, and crime indicate that the moral fiber of America has been weakened. They indicate too that we Christians have not done our job. We need to become aware of the "signs of the times," and do something about them.

I have met kids who smoke grass in church parlors and have "beer busts" to raise funds for "spiritual" retreats. Kids involved in this kind of stuff have heard enough of the Gospel to turn them off—but not enough to turn them on.

Of course there are some church members, and even some ministers, who don't believe Jesus is the answer to the world's problems. These are the humanists who put their faith in man's ability to do it all himself. To them, the savior of the world is social action.

One day a stranger came up to me at the filling station where I was having my car serviced. "Hey," he said, "aren't you the guy working with that new kid group?"

"Yes, I am," I acknowledged.

"I want to talk to you sometime soon," he said. "When do you have time?"

We agreed to meet for lunch the next Wednesday.

When I entered the cafe at the appointed time, I found two men waiting for me. After we had ordered, they asked me to explain what I was "trying to do with kids."

It took me a while to catch on to the fact that both of them were ministers. It's hard to tell sometimes. But I proceeded to explain Young Life's program.

Impatiently, one of the men asked me,—and by now I realized that both of them were ministers—"Do you subscribe to the five-point doctrine that Young Life believes in?"

Without hesitation, I said, "If you mean, do I believe in the Bible—yes!"

This man didn't like that answer. "In your own words, tell us what you are really trying to get kids to do," he said.

"Basically, we ask kids to give their lives to Jesus Christ—to surrender to Him."

The minister blew up. "That's what I thought you guys were all about," he snorted. "Look, you don't seem like a dumb bunny. You have an

173

education. You've been around some. How can you—a young, well-rounded person—how can you believe all that——? You must know better!"

With some other choice words that cannot be published, he pursued his argument that grown people mature. They get out of the simple, narrow, Christian bag and into the real stuff: social action.

Once in a great while, I blow *my* cool. This was one of those times. As much as I wanted to express love and restrain myself, I had to let it all out: "You call yourselves ministers of the Gospel of Jesus Christ, and yet you don't believe in Him or in His power to save?"

"We used to," one of them replied. "We were once caught in that narrow bag, but we've grown out of it. That 'me and Jesus' stuff has got to go."

The other man echoed, "Yeah, it's got to go."

In a belated attempt not to antagonize these influential men, I told them that I understood their indictment of Christians who say a lot but do little, and I thought the indictment was a fair one. We discussed that issue for quite awhile.

"But I have one serious question I would like to ask you," I went on, turning to the younger of the two men. "How can you continue to call your church a Christian church (not the real name) when you feel this way? Aren't you being unfair to your people?"

"We need that name because people understand it," was the reply. "They can identify with it. We need that name because it draws people to us so that we can teach them about life. It would be unfair for us to change it now. These people are too familiar with it."

As I stood up to leave, I told them both that I thought they should be honest enough to change their church signs to read, "The Church of Activists."

The encounter with those two ministers really shook me up. I was aware that some members of the clergy were not completely on target, but I had never before had a minister deny the very central core of Christian belief. That conversation challenged me to get moving. "If churches aren't proclaiming the Good News in full," I said to myself, "then I have all the more responsibility for getting it across to kids."

Over this and many other situations I encounter in my ministry, I have cried out to God. Being with kids who are dying inside, with married couples on the verge of divorce, with families in despair about their lost children ... listening to daily news reports ... spending months in high school and college corridors ... watching Christian kids step into secular traps

. . . church services that are plastic and phony —all these have compelled me to get on my knees to plead with God.

In many of the cases I deal with, prayer is my *only* recourse. These are situations in which action—social and otherwise—is in vain. I have learned that prayer *is* "the mightiest force in the world," as Dr. Frank Laubach called it in the title of his book. It works powerfully and swiftly, changing circumstances, changing attitudes (mine and other people's,) communicating love, reaching into the depths of people's hearts and minds, to renew them and transform their lives.

The question is, knowing this, why do we Christians who *know* the power of prayer spend so little time doing it? Many of us spend three to five hours a day watching television, yet we refuse to give God even *one* hour.

For many months Mary Beth and I, after watching the network television coverage of the daily news, were sunk in gloom over the terrible situation the world is in. Finally it dawned on us that we had a responsibility to do something more positive about that situation. Now, as we watch the daily newscast, we pray about each situation as it is presented, and pray for the announcer and the commentator. We use the negative news as a stimulant to positive action— prayer. Whatever effect our prayers are having on world events, they are making us more aware of our adult responsibility to tell today's generation that Jesus Christ is the answer to all these complicated problems—and the answer to all our smaller problems too!

Chapter 13

The hill, though high, I covet to ascend,
The difficulty will not me offend;
For I perceive the way to life lies here.
Come, pluck up heart, let's neither faint
                    nor fear;
Better, though difficult, the right way to go,
Than wrong, though easy, where the end is woe.

> *The Pilgrim's Progress*
> John Bunyan,
> Rinehart Editions
> P. 43

Someone to Love Them

A unique privilege has been mine for the past eighteen months—that of sitting on the State Board of Pardons with three of the most influential men in the state of North Dakota: the governor, the attorney general, and the chief justice of the supreme court. These men are compassionate, concerned, loving servants, who truly care about what happens to the inmates in the state prison, as well as other constituents in their state.

At one of our recent meetings, thirty-five candidates for pardon had to be interviewed. None of these interviews was routine, but one of them developed into a dialogue of real significance.

A young pardon candidate named Richard requested a commutation of his sentence on the premise that he was not guilty of his original charge. Since being in prison, however, he had added fifteen years to his sentence by attempting to escape, smuggling dope into the prison, and breaking other prison regulations. As is often the case, one bad break had led to another. We all listened intently as Richard spoke.

"I know you men won't grant my request. I can feel it. You think I'm a bad ——, just like everybody else does. I don't stand a chance of ever making it in life. How can I, when everyone is against me? I don't stand a chance."

Perspiration began to appear on Richard's brow as he continued to verbalize his hostility: "Since I won't get a pardon, I might as well lay it on you exactly the way it is. You dumb ——s don't know what's going on. You don't see how bad things are. You don't realize that we are just a few steps away from revolution in this country. This whole —— system is —— up. Nothing can change it. It's corrupt to the core.

"Someday soon," he continued, "the whole —— world is going to blow up right before your —— eyes. Then you'll learn!"

I had heard this sort of talk from many alienated kids, and I felt a real empathy for this alienated prisoner who was little more than a kid himself.

"Richard," I asked, "what would it take to help you?"

"You wanna change me? You want me to be different? For what? Who cares about whether I change or not? Even though I'm miserable the way I am, I like it this way. I enjoy being ornery. Why the hell do you ask?"

"Richard," I said, "we want you to be free just a much as you want to be. But it's obvious that something has to happen to you before you can get out." Knowing that Richard had been given all the psychiatric, psychological, and sociologic help available in the prison system, I asked again, "Really, Richard, deep down in your guts, what would it take to make you more accepting, more willing to cooperate with others?"

Tense silence filled the room as tears began to roll down Richard's cheeks. His head was hanging, his hands tightly clenched. Slowly he lifted his head and began speaking softly, as if every bit of violence within him had been drained.

"I need a break. . . ." he paused. "I need someone to love me. I need someone to care enough about me to reach inside my guts." As the tears flowed more freely, he continued, "If I knew that just one person loved me, I could change. I don't have anyone. No one. No one at all. Can you understand that? I don't really want to be this way. I really don't. I'm sorry."

As I looked over Richard's record, I understood what he was saying. His parents had abandoned him when he was a baby, and he had been raised in orphanages and boarding schools. His first arrest came when he was fifteen, and three of his high school years had been spent in a state reform school.

After a few other questions, Richard was excused from the Pardon Board Hearing Room. As he started to leave, I felt impelled to speak to him again.

"Richard," I said, "believe me. We care about you—and I know Someone else Who does too."

His eyes lit up as he looked at me. "Who?" he asked.

"As stupid as it may sound, Richard, I want you to know that Jesus cares about you. Will you give Him a chance? He'll help you." After some hesitation, Richard nodded and left the room.

Frequently, at night and during my early morning prayer times, I see Richard's face before me—his and the faces of numerous other inmates, kids, and hurting people.

So little is being done for these sufferers. There are so many hurts and so few to bind up the wounds and to minister the love of Jesus.

In a sense, *we* put Richard and those other men where they are. More than ninety percent of prison inmates in North Dakota come from adoptive, alcoholic, Indian, underprivileged, or broken homes. They are sentenced to terms extending from one year to life.

What can I do for these men and women? How can I reach the young people who've gone bad? I lie awake at night trying to devise a plan for ministering to the inmates of our prison system. Something *must* be done.

I literally weep when I think of the large numbers of families that have been torn apart by the imprisonment of one of their members. Some of my tears are tears of penitence—for I realize that I have a share of responsibility for the ills of this world.

I know there is only one cure for those ills—and that is *love*. Yet I know that I am incapable of loving *anyone*—much less criminals—until I allow God's love to flow through me. Only God can give me the love, the perseverance, the plan for reaching others, and the compassion and understanding so desperately needed by alienated members of our society—whether rebellious kids or hardened criminals.

There are many service organizations reaching out sporadically in an effort to heal the hurts of the world: to feed the hungry, to clothe the naked, to visit the sick and those in prison. But it is only we as individuals in our own denominations, and the church as a whole, that can do the complete job of ministering to the physical, emotional, and spiritual needs of all humanity. Such a tremendous task can be accomplished only by the *whole* Church—the body of Christ in the world—through the power, wisdom, and love of the Holy Spirit.

*There are three grand essentials
to happiness in this
life.
They are . . .
something to do,
something to love,
something to hope for.*

—Joseph Addison

Let him that would move
the world,
first
move himself.

—Socrates

*An
experience-centered
book, like the
Christian life,
has no ending.*

INSPIRATIONAL PAPERBACKS
FROM WHITAKER HOUSE

THE ACTS OF THE GREEN APPLES
by Jean Stone Willans $1.45

Today soldiers, sailors, priests, nuns, Chinese, Americans, Englishmen, and others of all descriptions flock to the Willanses' miracle-studded mission in Hong Kong. But it wasn't always so. Once upon a time, the Willanses were quiet, respectable suburbanites. The story of how they got to Hong Kong is the heart-warming, miracle-studded and frankly hilarious account of THE ACTS OF THE GREEN APPLES.

CLIMB MOUNT MORIAH
by Pat Brooks $1.25

A fascinating study of people who have passed through life's darkest moments, facing prospects of broken marriage and adultery, financial ruin and disgrace. They learned how to tap vast reservoirs of spiritual power and come through to victory—and so can you!

FAITH UNDER FIRE
by Chris Panos $ .95

Learn the secrets of fiery faith, as Chris Panos shares with you the insights that have enabled him to heal the sick, win thousands of souls to

Christ, and smuggle Bibles into Iron and Bamboo Curtain countries at the risk of his life.

GILLIES' GUIDE TO HOME PRAYER MEETINGS
by George and Harriet Gillies $1.25

He is a retired Wall Street executive. She is his wife. Together, they wrote *A Scriptural Outline of the Baptism in the Holy Spirit*. Now the Gillies bring us this practical, step-by-step handbook dealing with the problems and procedures involved in setting up the kind of home fellowship that will bless the lives of all attending.

IF I CAN, YOU CAN
by Betty Lee Esses $2.25

The wife of charismatic teacher Michael Esses tells how Jesus saved her husband and her marriage and shares what He's been teaching the Esses ever since. For Betty, these were hard-won spiritual insights. For you, they can come easy; all you have to do is read this book.

IF YOU SEE LENNIE
by Char Potterbaum $1.45

Once upon a time, Char Potterbaum was so full of tranquilizers, pepper-uppers, and other pills that her husband claimed she rattled when she turned over in bed. Learn why she doesn't need pills anymore—and how she exchanged her depression for joy—in a book that combines everyday, homespun humor with true spiritual wisdom.

A MANUAL ON EXORCISM
by H. A. Maxwell Whyte $1.25

The *Exorcist* posed the question; this book has the answers. Are there really such things as demons?

How can you know if you have one? How do you get rid of them? When demons talk, whose voice do they use? Can anybody cast out demons? How do you go about it? These and many more troublesome questions are clearly answered in this helpful book.

THE NEW WINE IS BETTER
by Robert Thom $1.45

Anyone with problems (and who hasn't got problems?) needs to read this story of one man who saw the invisible, believed the incredible, and received the impossible. A lively and often amusing account of Robert Thom's downward trek from a 12 bedroom mansion in South Africa to the hopeless world of an alcoholic on the verge of suicide—and a whole new world of faith and power Robert Thom discovered after Mrs. Webster came knocking on his door.

PLEASE MAKE ME CRY!
by Cookie Rodriguez $1.45

The first female dope addict to "kick the habit" in Dave Wilkerson's ministry, Cookie was so hard people said even death didn't want her. Told the way it really happened, this is the explosive, exciting, sometimes shocking—but always true—story of how Cookie found Someone she wanted even more than heroin.

THERE'S DYNAMITE IN PRAISE
by Don Gossett $1.25

Here's how to get your prayers answered—and then some! Learn how even seemingly horrible circumstances can be used by God for your benefit and how to unlock God's best for you, in a manual designed to lead you into a new and power-packed relationship with Him.

WHEREVER PAPERBACKS ARE SOLD
OR USE THIS COUPON

Whitaker House

504 LAUREL DRIVE, MONROEVILLE, PA 15146

SEND INSPIRATIONAL BOOKS LISTED BELOW.

Title	Price	☐ Send Complete Catalog
_____	_____	
_____	_____	
_____	_____	
_____	_____	
_____	_____	
_____	_____	
_____	_____	
_____	_____	

Name_____

Street_____

City_____State_____Zip_____